Great Fiddling Tunes

Early Music Gems

by Craig Duncan

Online Audio

To access the online audio go to:
WWW.MELBAY.COM/30815MEB

WWW.MELBAY.COM

Preface

Early Music Gems contains 49 melodies that date from 1300 – 1791. Many of the tunes come from the English Country Dance tradition and are useful today for Country Dance and Contradance settings as well as for concerts. Medieval, Renaissance, early classical and ancient Christmas melodies round out the collection. Suggested bowings, chords and tempos are included.

Most of the melodies are in alphabetical order. One exception is *Bonny Kate*, which is paired with *Harper's Frolic* as the two are often played as a set. Several of the tunes have more than one name.

Includes access to an online audio recording of the fiddle melody with guitar accompaniment of each of the tunes. These recordings will aid in learning the styles and nuances of the tunes.

May you enjoy bringing these historic melodies to life.

Index

Title		Page	Audio
All You That Are Good Fellows	*Christmas Carol 1642*	4	1
Alman – Allmayne	*Robert Johnson (1583-1633)*	6	2
An Italian Rant – La Montovana	*John Playford 1657*	7	3
Bar A Bar	*English Country Dance*	8	4
Bobbing Joe	*John Playford*	8	5
Black Nag – The Galloping Nag	*John Playford 1670*	9	6
Blessed Be That Maid Marie	*Ballet's Lute Book 1600*	10	7
Bonnie Kate	*Morris Dance*	26	21
Bransle Double – from *Terpsichore*	*Michael Praetorious 1612*	11	8
Canarios	*Gaspar Sanz (1640-1710)*	12	9
Chestnut	*John Playford 1670*	14	10
Childgrove	*John Playford 1701*	15	11
Come With Me, My Giselle	*Adam de la Halle 13th Century*	16	12
Confess (His Tune) – The Court Lady	*English Dance Tune 1650*	17	13
The Cutty Wren	*Traditional English*	41	41
Dont vient cela	*Tielman Susato (1510-1570)*	18	14
Duke of Kent's Waltz	*English Country Dance*	19	15
Drive the Cold Winter Away	*John Playford*	20	16
Fortune My Foe	*16th Century*	22	17
Greensleeves	*Traditional English Ballad*	23	18
Grimstock	*John Playford 1651*	24	19
Harper's Frolic	*Morris Dance*	26	20
Heart's Ease	*Misogonus 1560*	27	22
Helas madame	*attributed to Henry VIII*	28	23
Highland Mary – Bamptom	*Morris Dance*	28	24
Hole in the Wall	*Henry Purcell (1659-1695)*	29	25
Hunsdon House	*John Playford 1670*	29	26
Jamaica – Jameko	*John Playford 1670*	30	27
Kemp's Jig	*English Country Dance 17th Century*	31	28
Kemp's Jig *Playford*	*John Playford 1651*	31	29
Juice of Barley – Cold and Raw the North Wind Doth Blow	*John Playford 1651, 1728*	32	30
Lilliburlero	*London 1661*	33	31
Man in the Moon	*Traditional English Waltz*	34	32
Newcastle	*John Playford 1651*	35	33
Packington's Pound	*16th Century English*	35	34
Off She Goes	*English Country Dance*	36	35
The Old Bachelor – Wells Humour	*Henry Purcell 1691*	37	36
Parson's Farewell	*John Playford 1651*	38	37
Portsmouth	*John Playford 1701*	39	38
Prince Rupert's March	*John Playford 1651*	40	40
Staines Morris	*Traditional English*	39	39
Rafe's Waltz	*Traditional English*	41	41
Salterello – Italiana	*Vincenzo Galilei (1520-1591)*	42	42
Scotch Cap – Edinburgh Castle	*John Playford 1651*	44	43
Sellenger's Round – The Beginning of the World	*16th Century William Byrd*	45	45
Step Stately – Jack Pudding	*English Country Dance*	46	46
Well Hall	*John Playford 1679*	47	47
Wilson's Wilde	*16th Century*	47	48
Westmorland – Westmoreland Waltz	*John Playford 1686*	48	49
Woodicock – Whirligig	*John Playford 1651*	44	44

All You That Are Good Fellows

Good and True, Fresh and New, Christmas Carols 1642

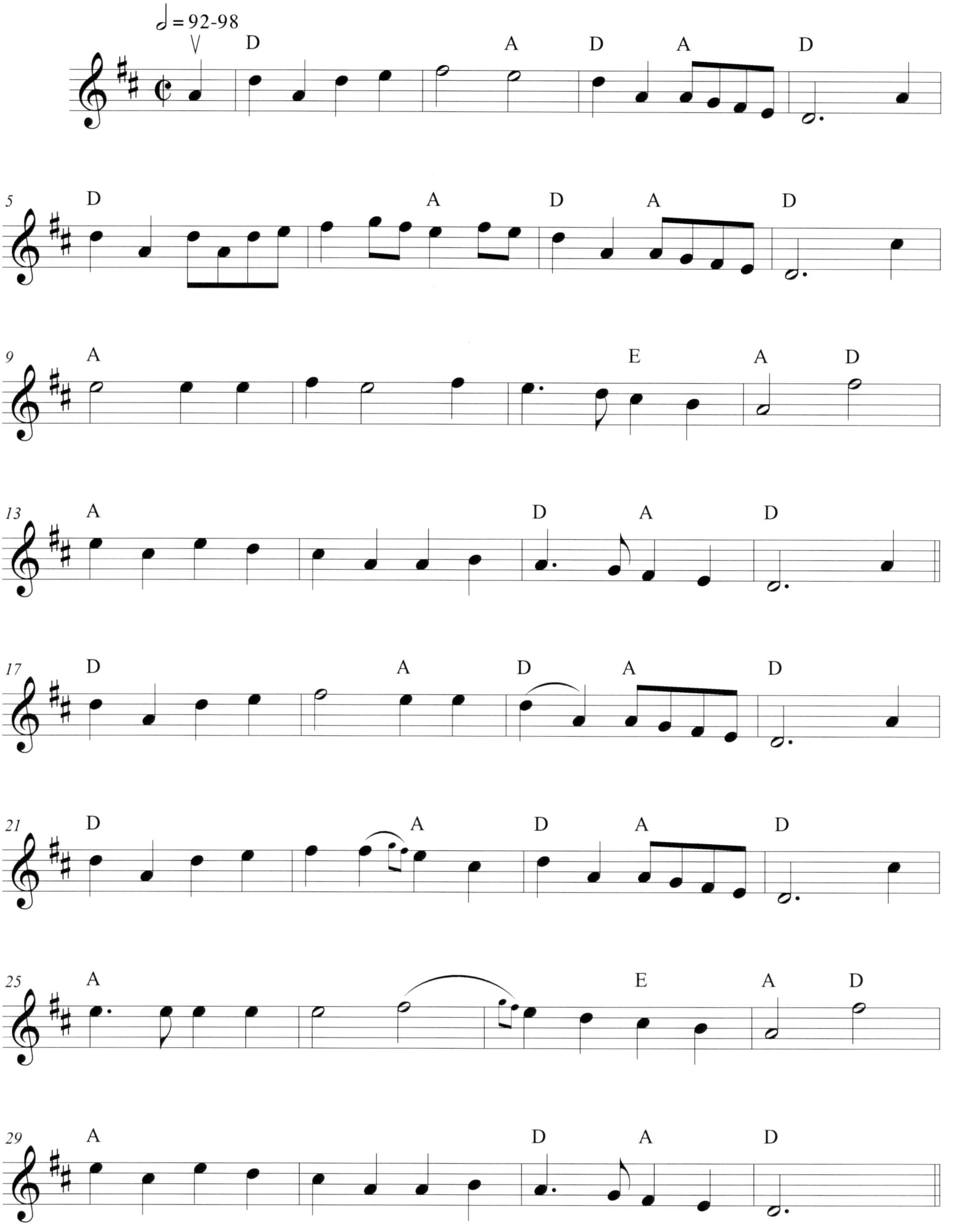

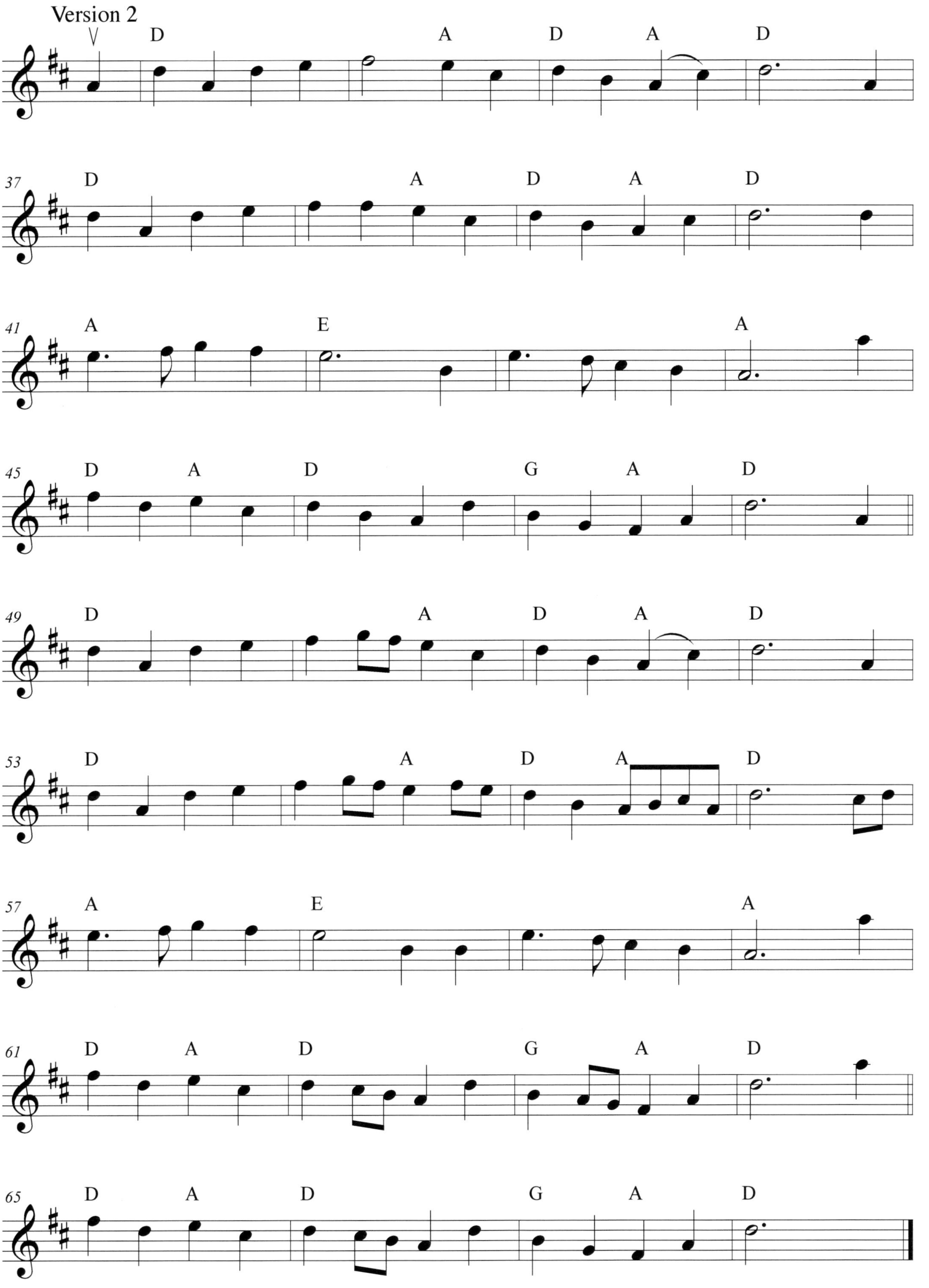
Version 2
D A D A D
D A D A D
A E A
D A D G A D
D A D A D
D A D A D
A E A
D A D G A D
D A D G A D

Alman

Allmayne

Robert Johnson (1583-1633)

Lightly ♩=100-106

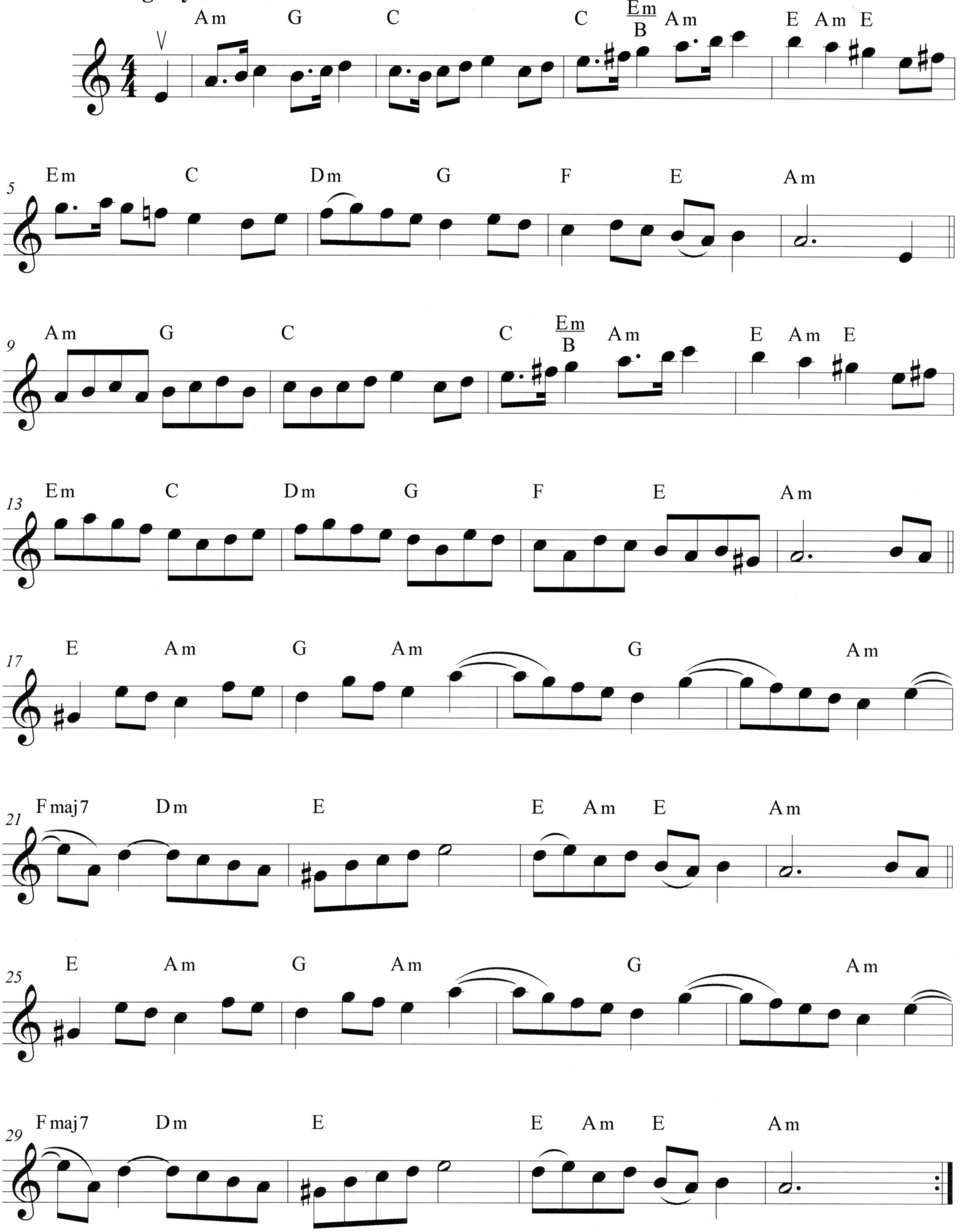

An Italian Rant

La Mantovana

𝅗𝅥 = 80-120

John Playford 1657

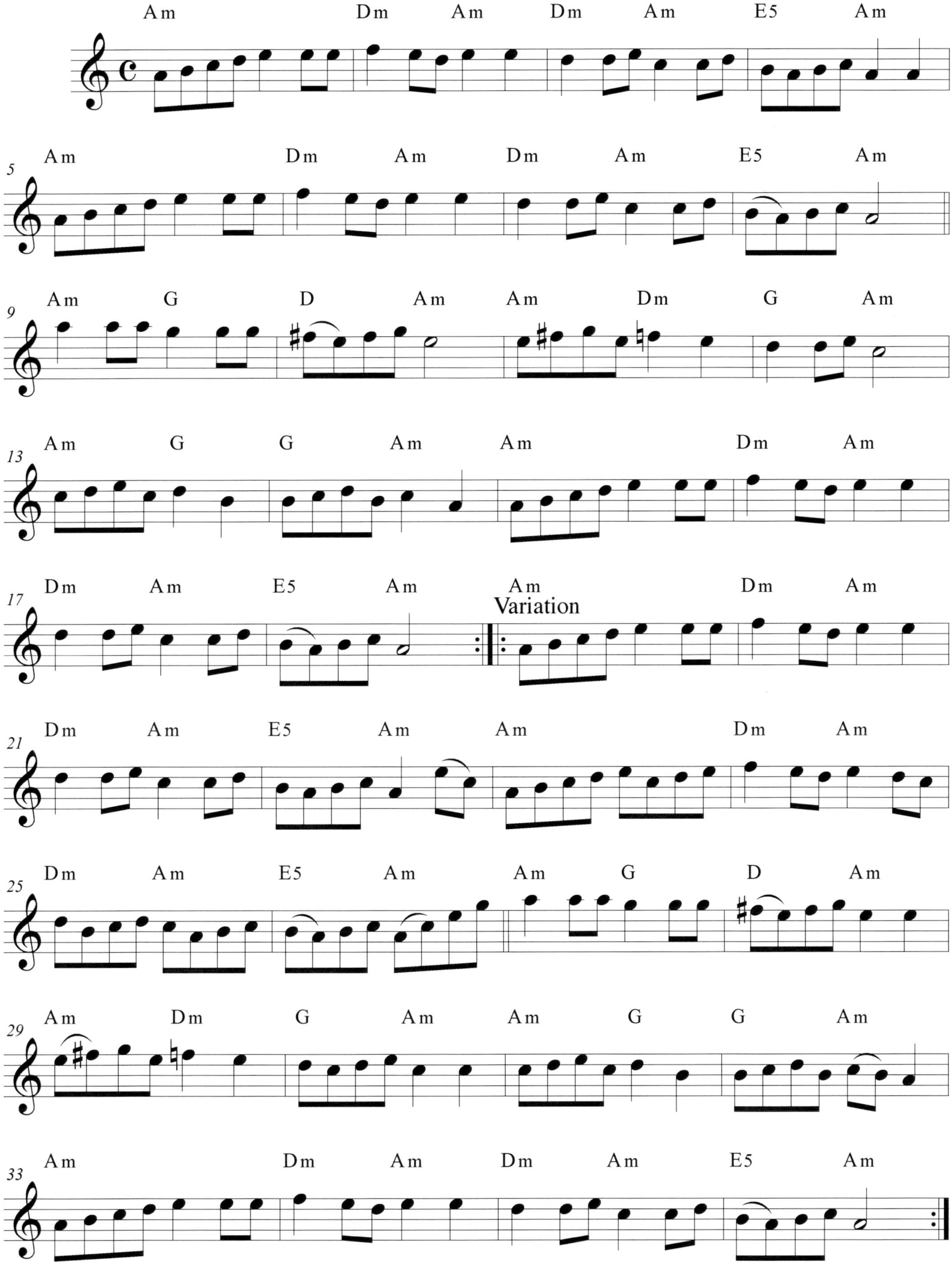

4

Bar A Bar

English Country Dance

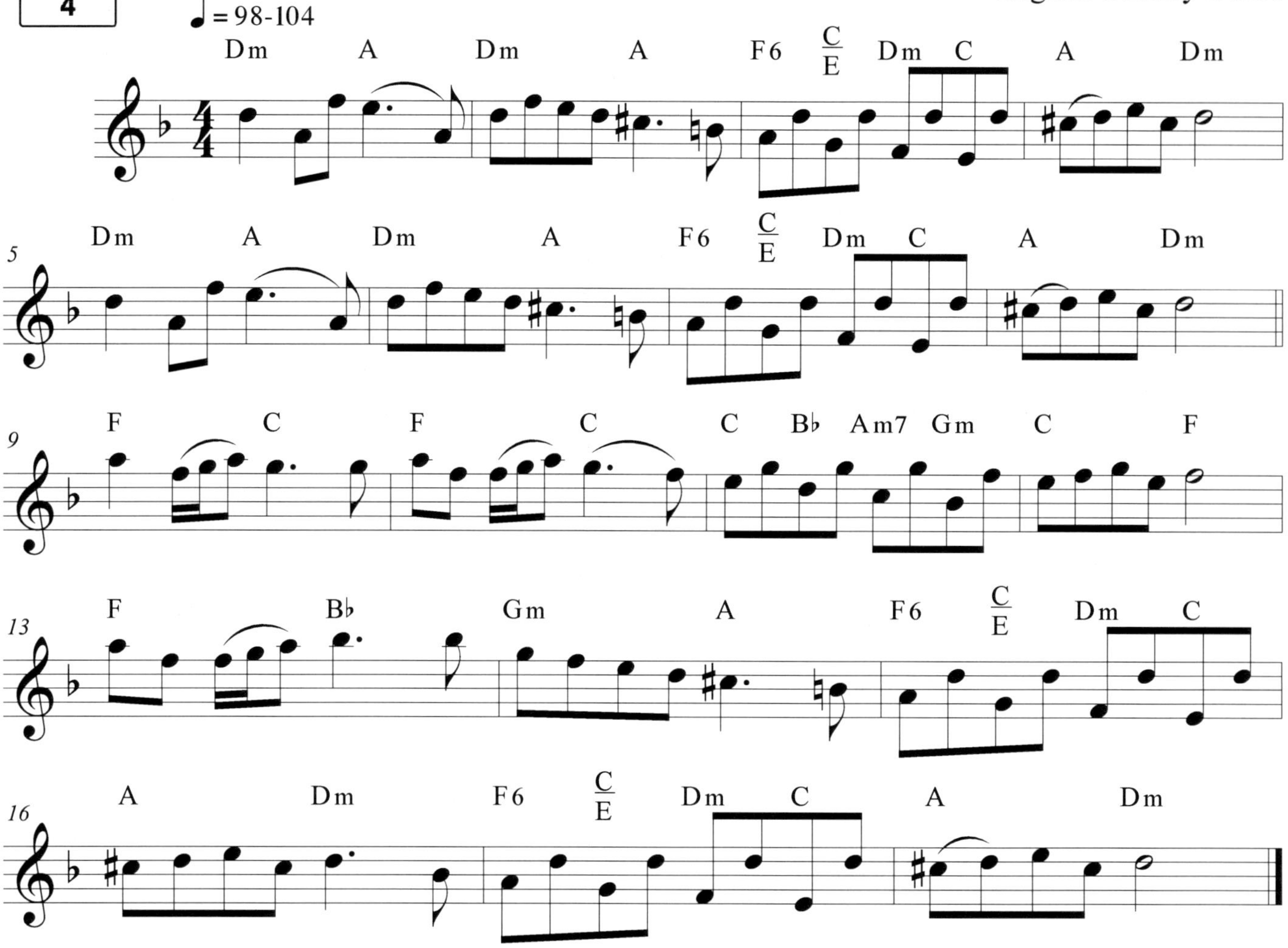

5

Bobbing Joe

John Playford

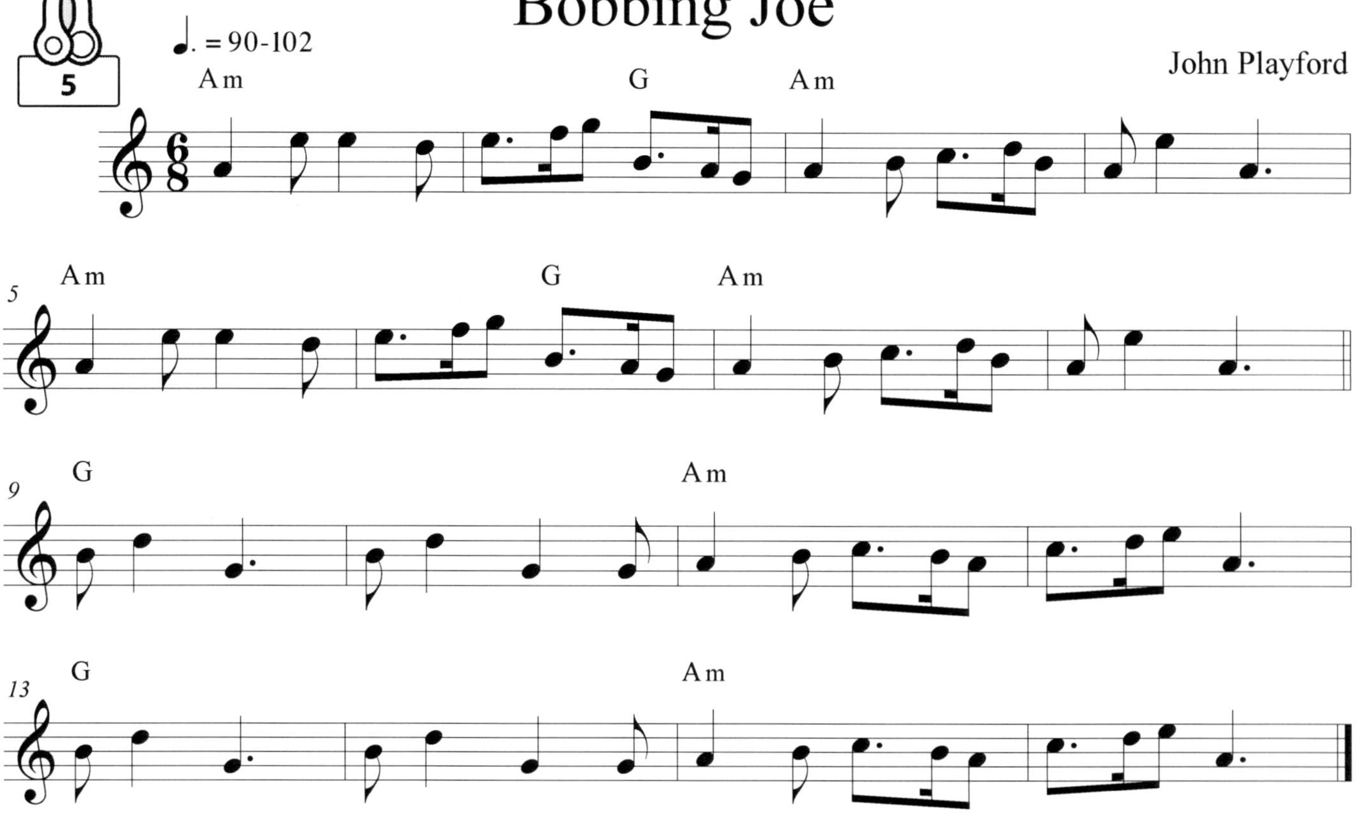

6

Black Nag

The Galloping Nag

John Playford 1670

♩. = 102-128

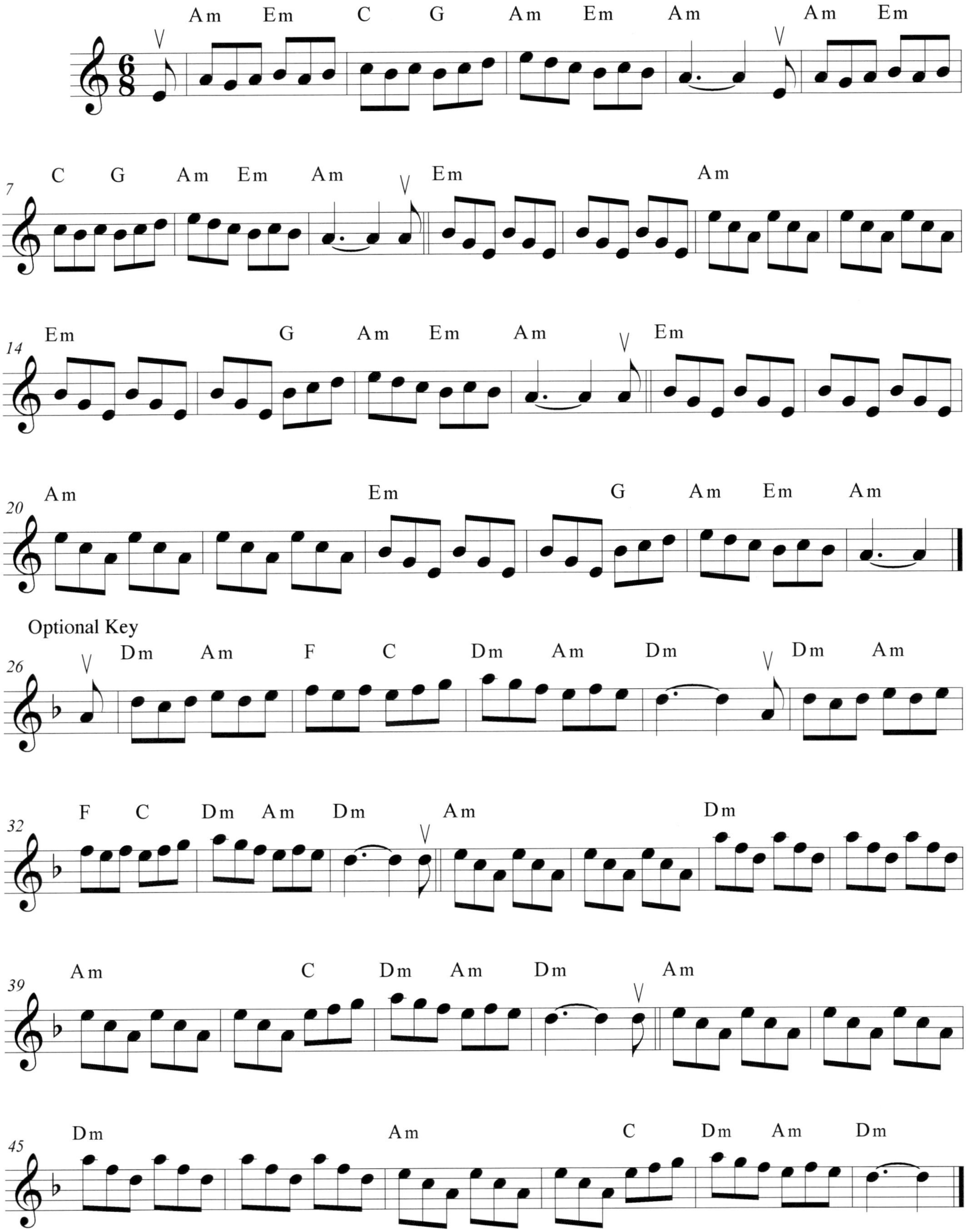

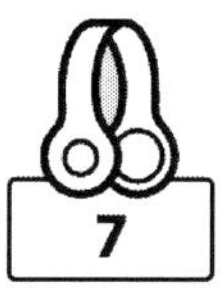

Blessed Be That Maid Marie

William Ballet's Lute Book 1600

𝅗𝅥 = 60-68

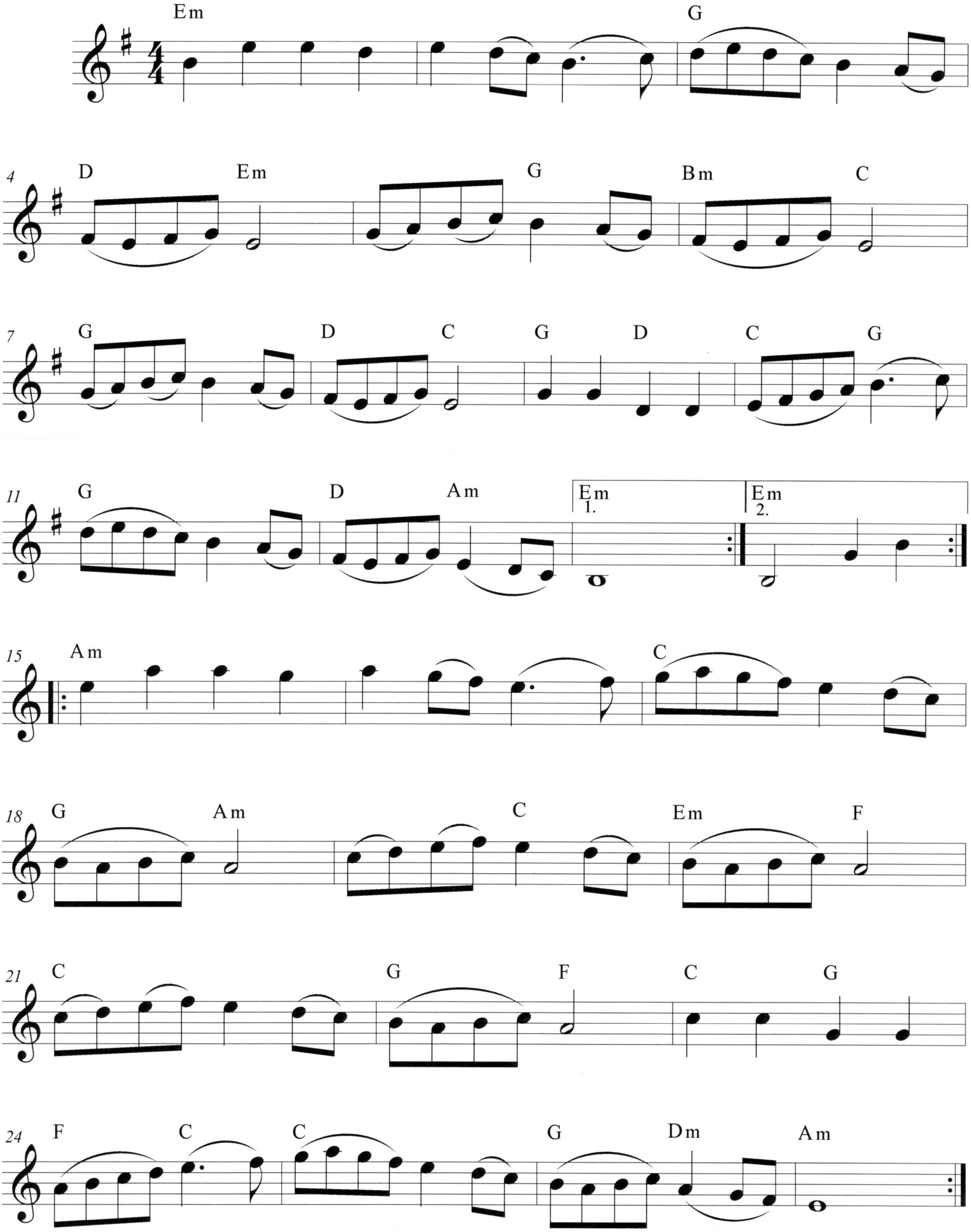

Bransle Double

from *Terpsichore*

Michael Praetorious 1612

Andante 𝅗𝅥=76-92

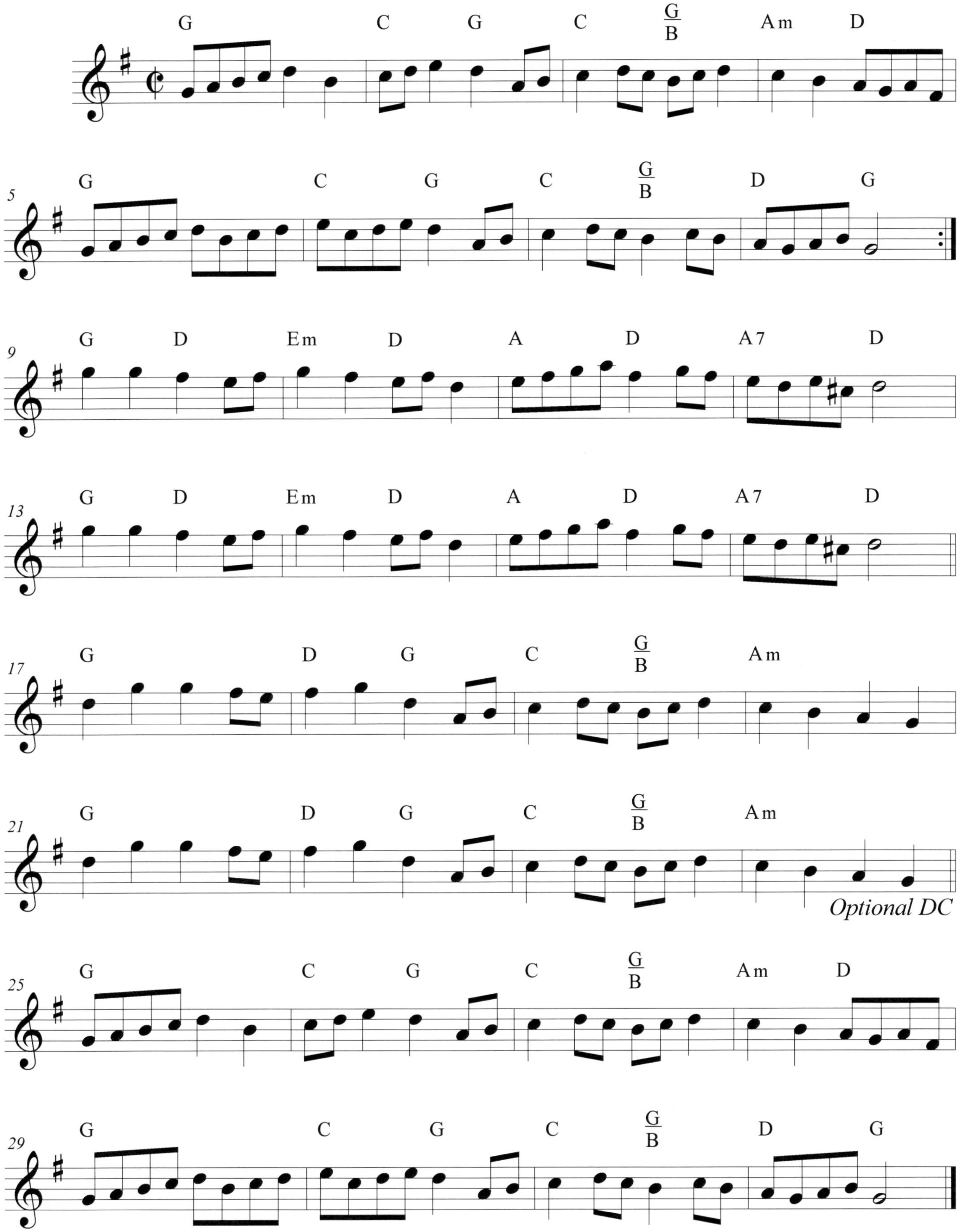

9

Canarios

Gaspar Sanz (1640-1710)

Lively ♩.=100-120

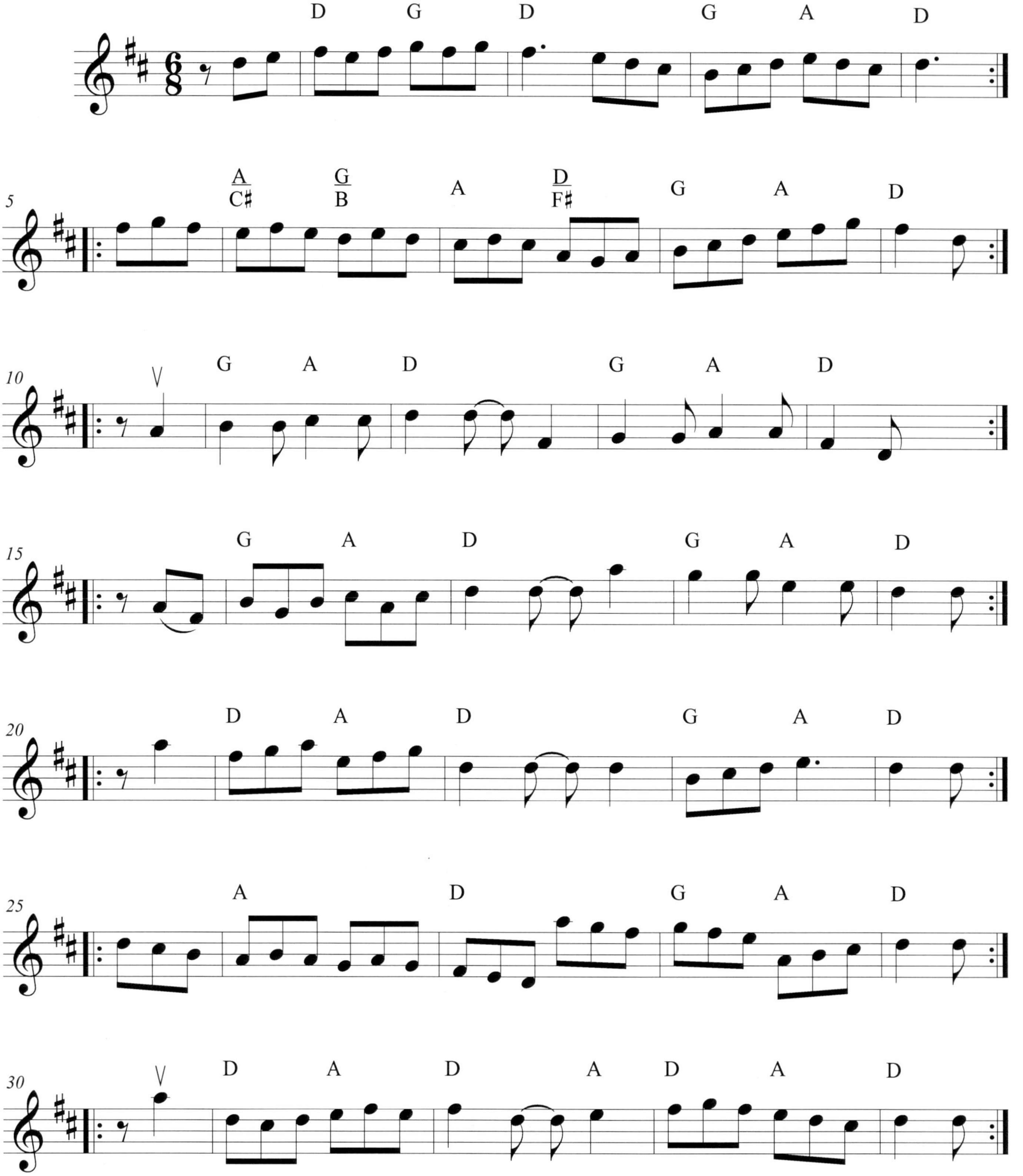

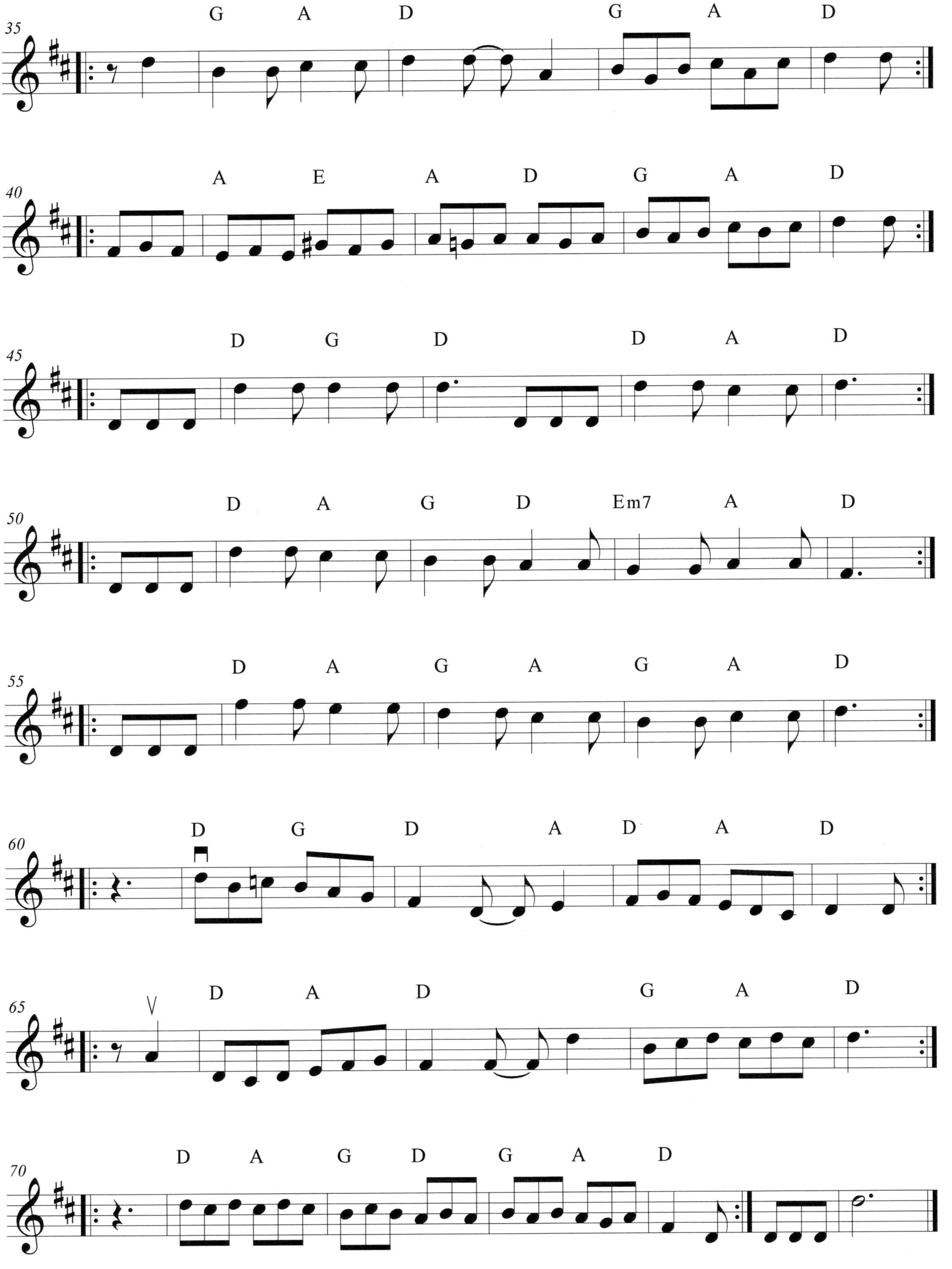
35
G A D G A D
40
A E A D G A D
45
D G D D A D
50
D A G D Em7 A D
55
D A G A G A D
60
D G D A D A D
65
D A D G A D
70
D A G D G A D

10

Chestnut

John Playford 1670

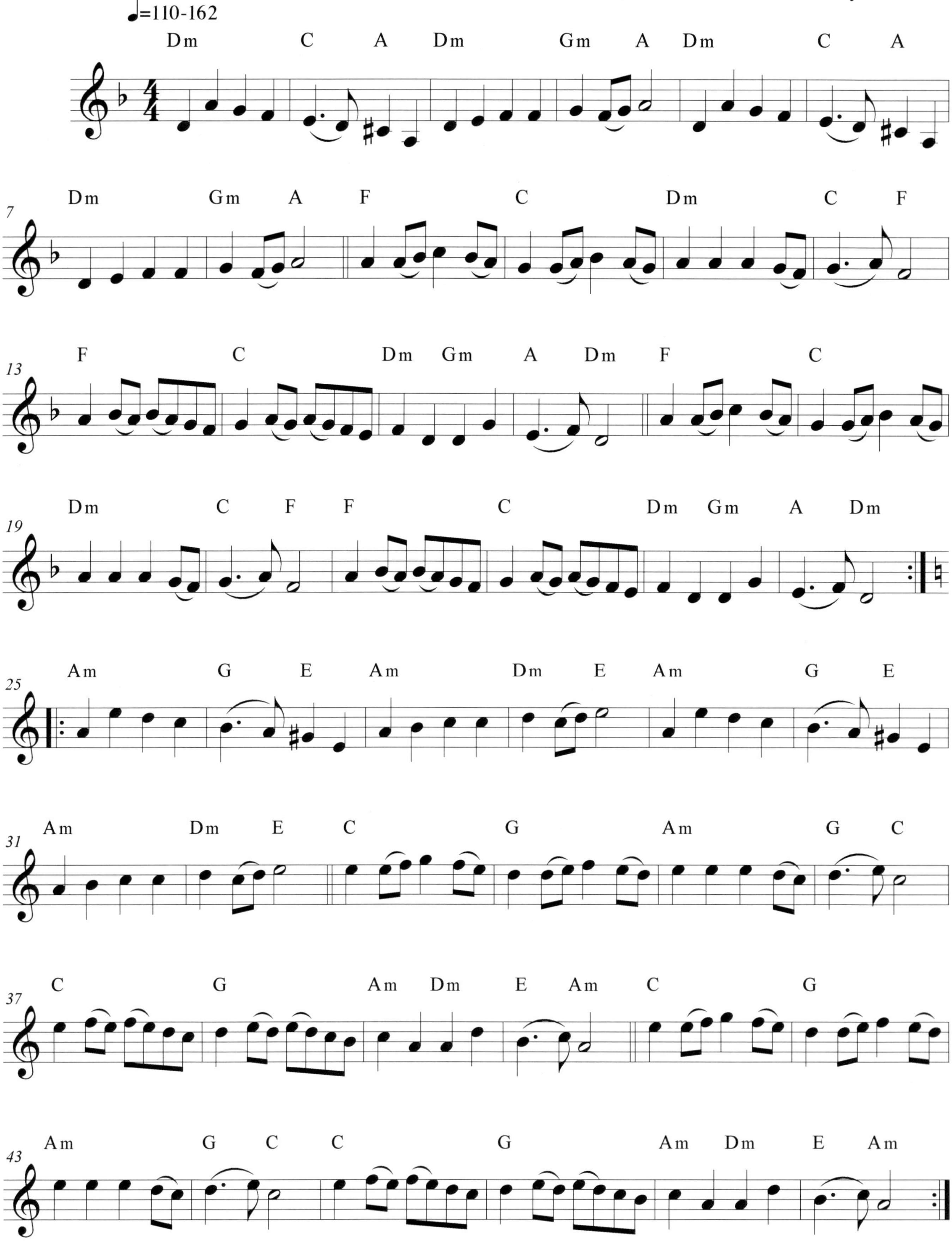

Chestnut is played both slowly as marked at 110 bpm and liltingly as marked at 162 bpm. This is sometimes done by changing tempos in the same performance.

11

Childgrove

John Playford 1701

♩ = 132-180

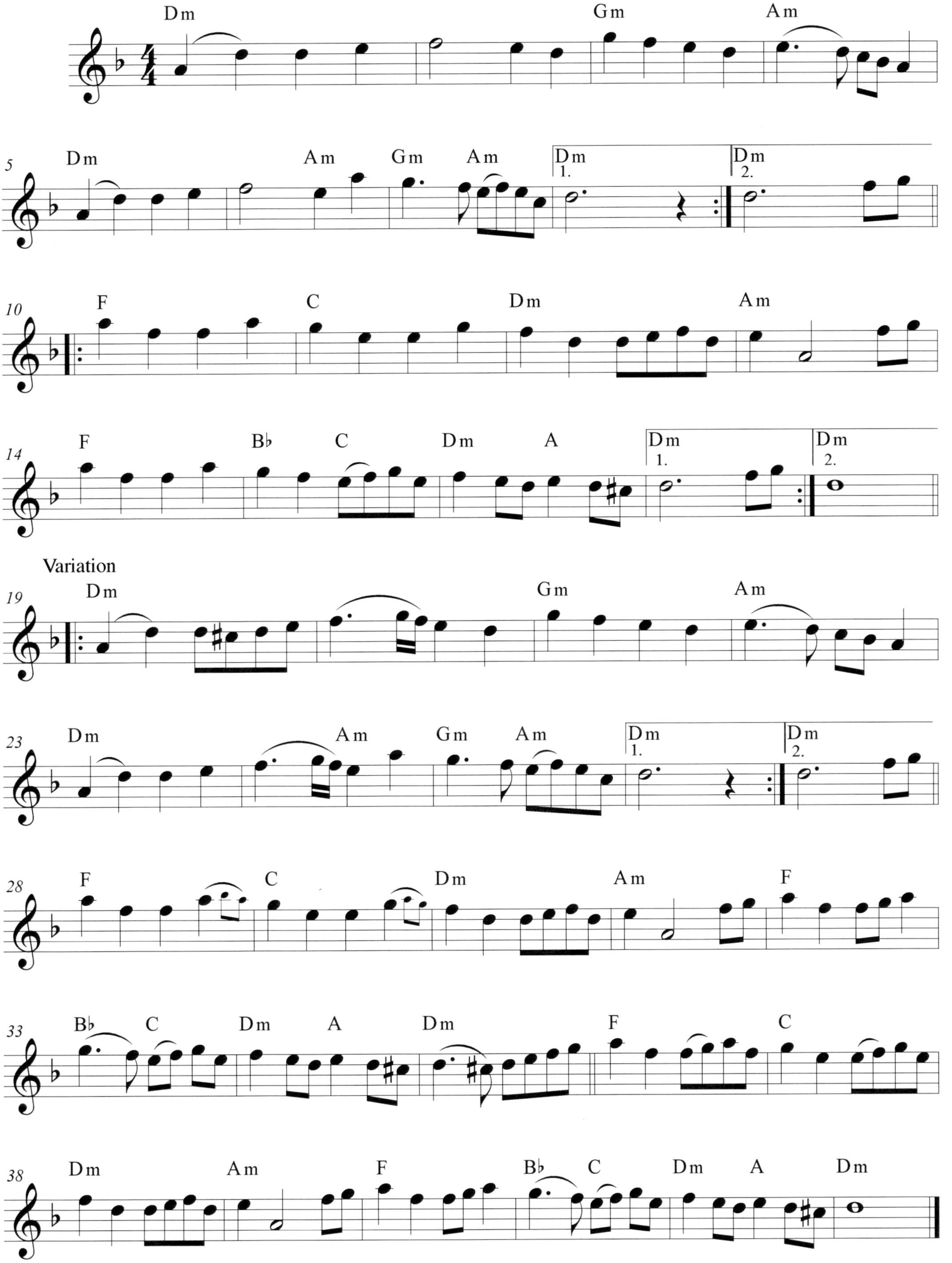

12

Come With Me, My Giselle

Gently ♩ = 90-98

Adam de la Halle 13th Century

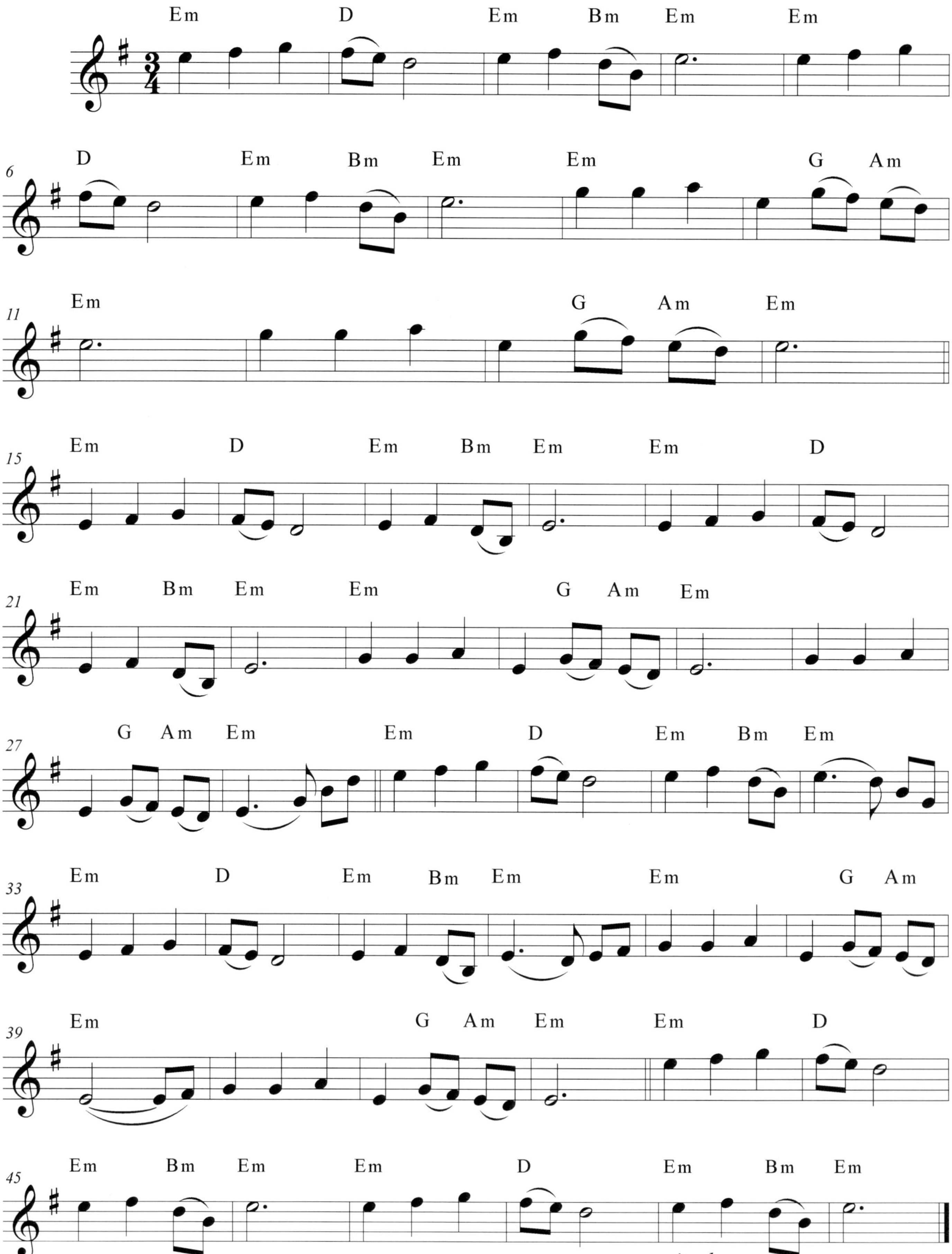

13

Confess (His Tune)

The Court Lady

English Dance Tune 1650

♩. = 92-98

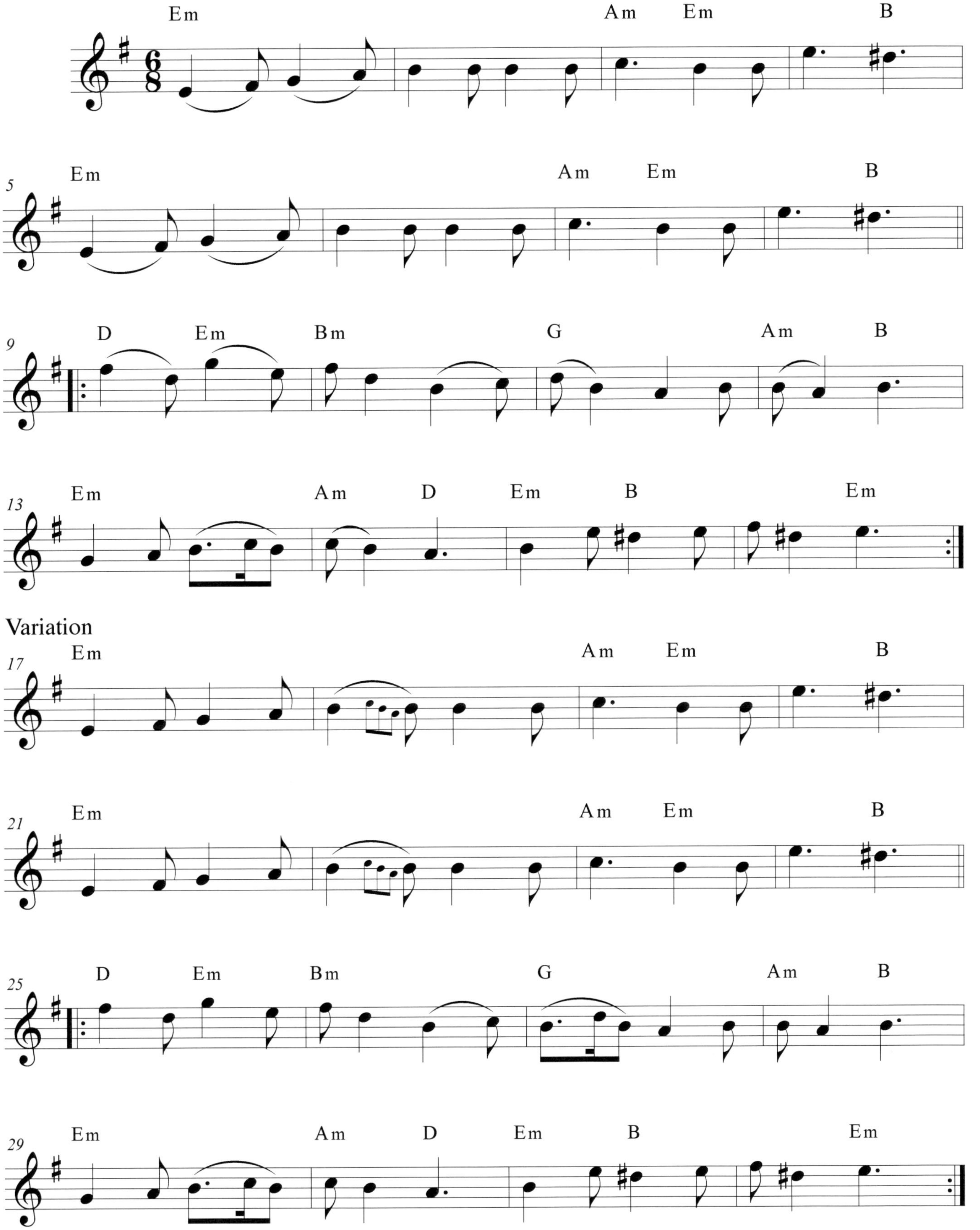

14

Dont vient cela

Tielman Susato (1510-1570)

𝅗𝅥. = 44-54 (♩ = 132-162)

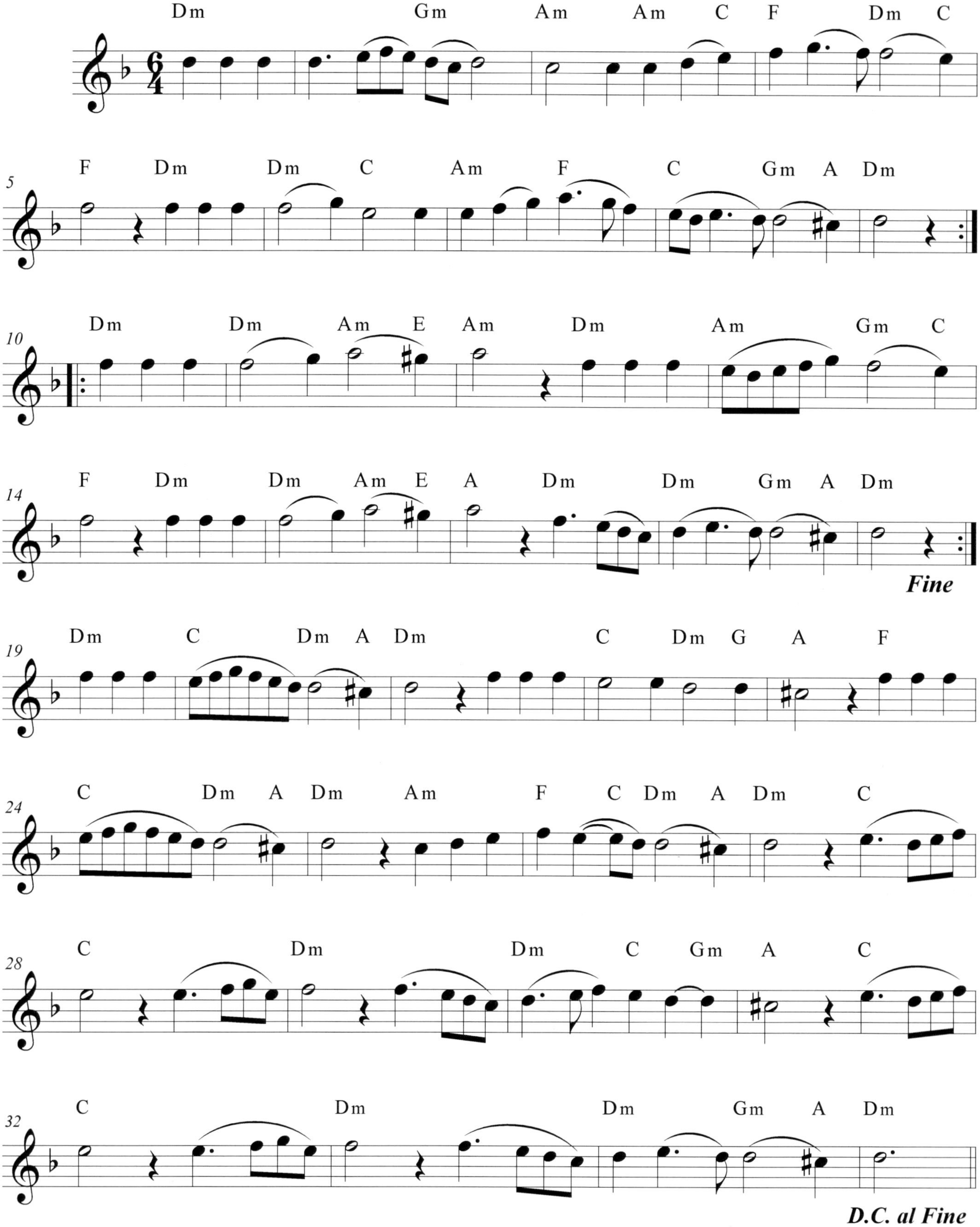

Duke of Kent's Waltz

English Country Dance

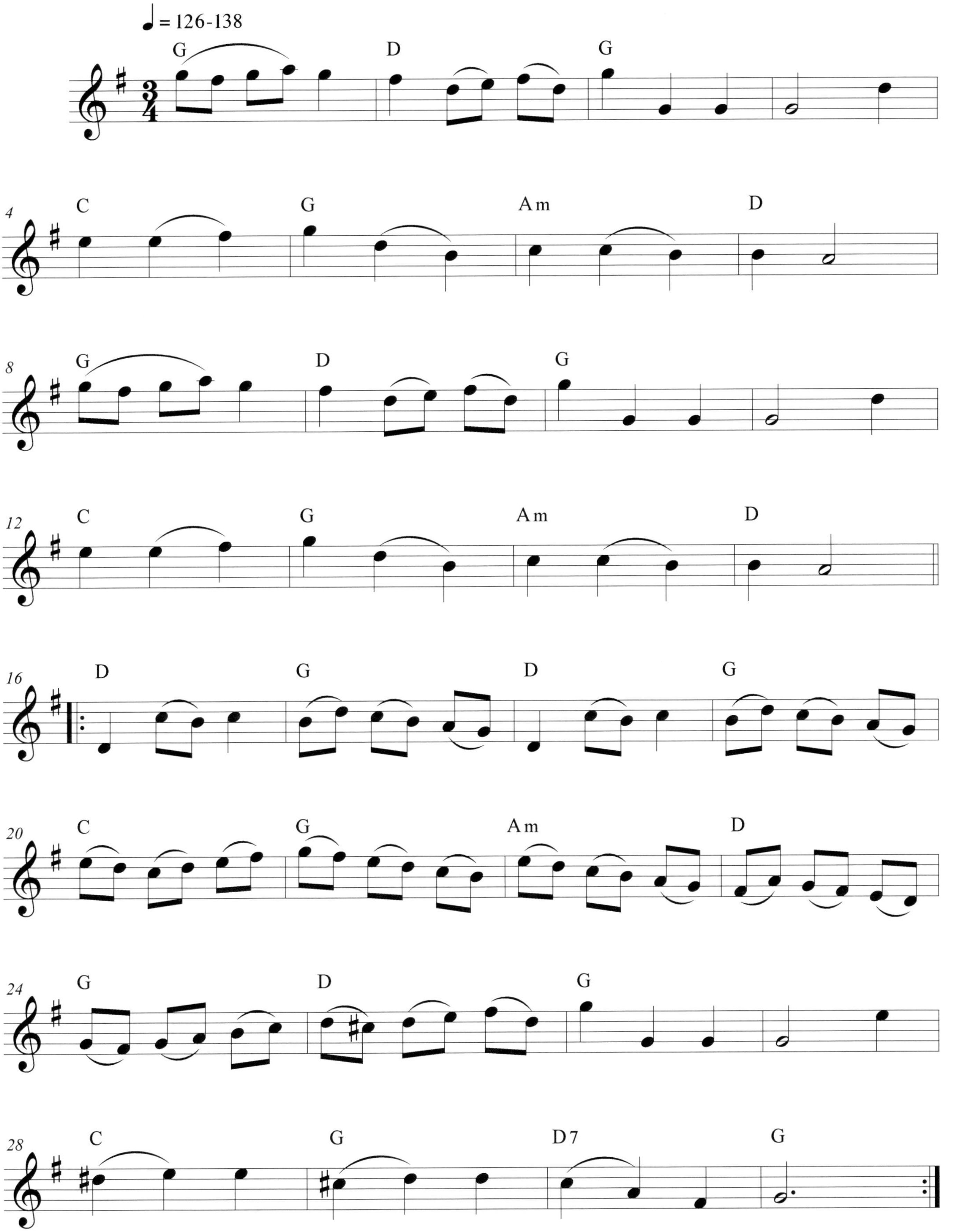

16

Drive the Cold Winter Away

John Playford

♩. = 60-70

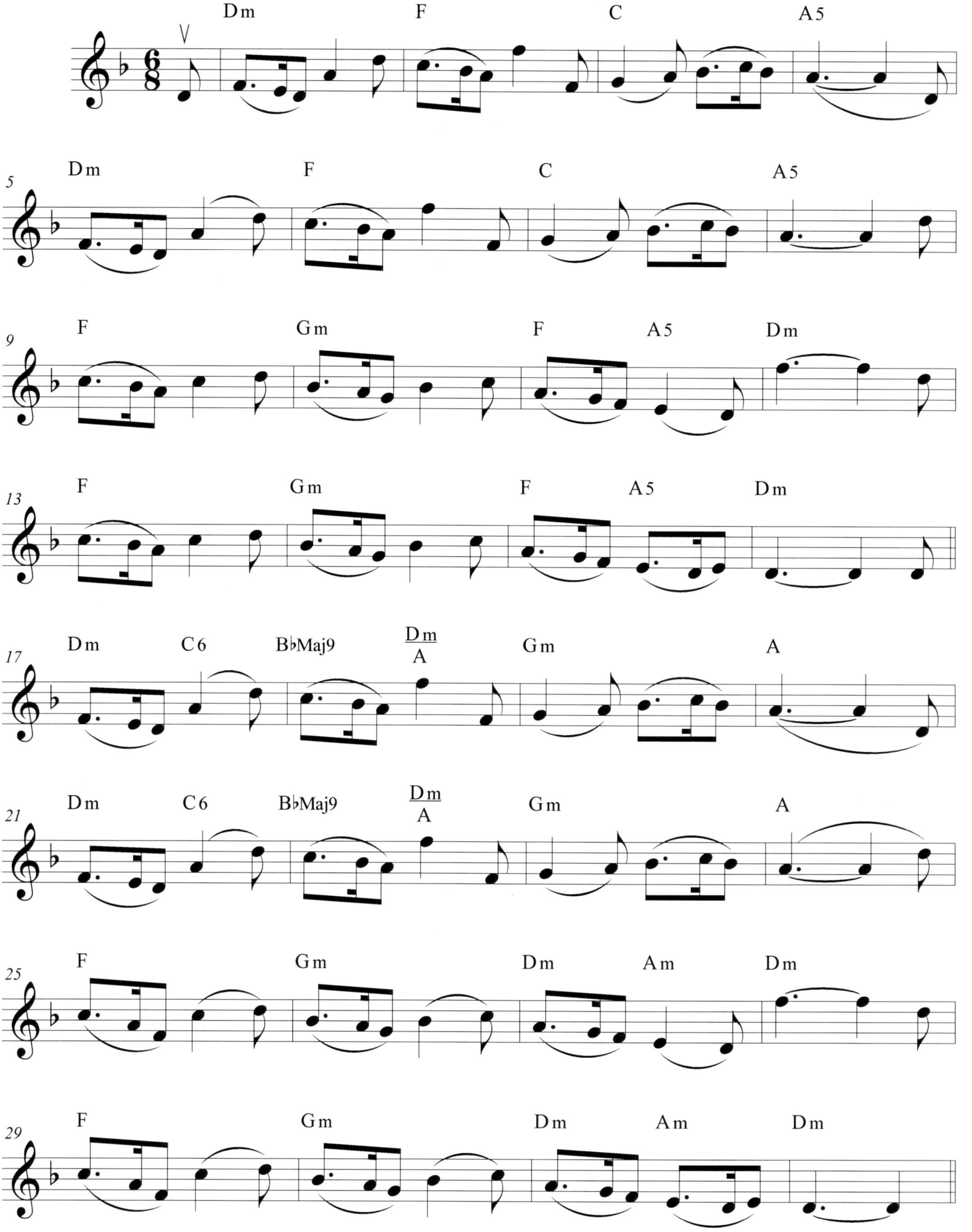

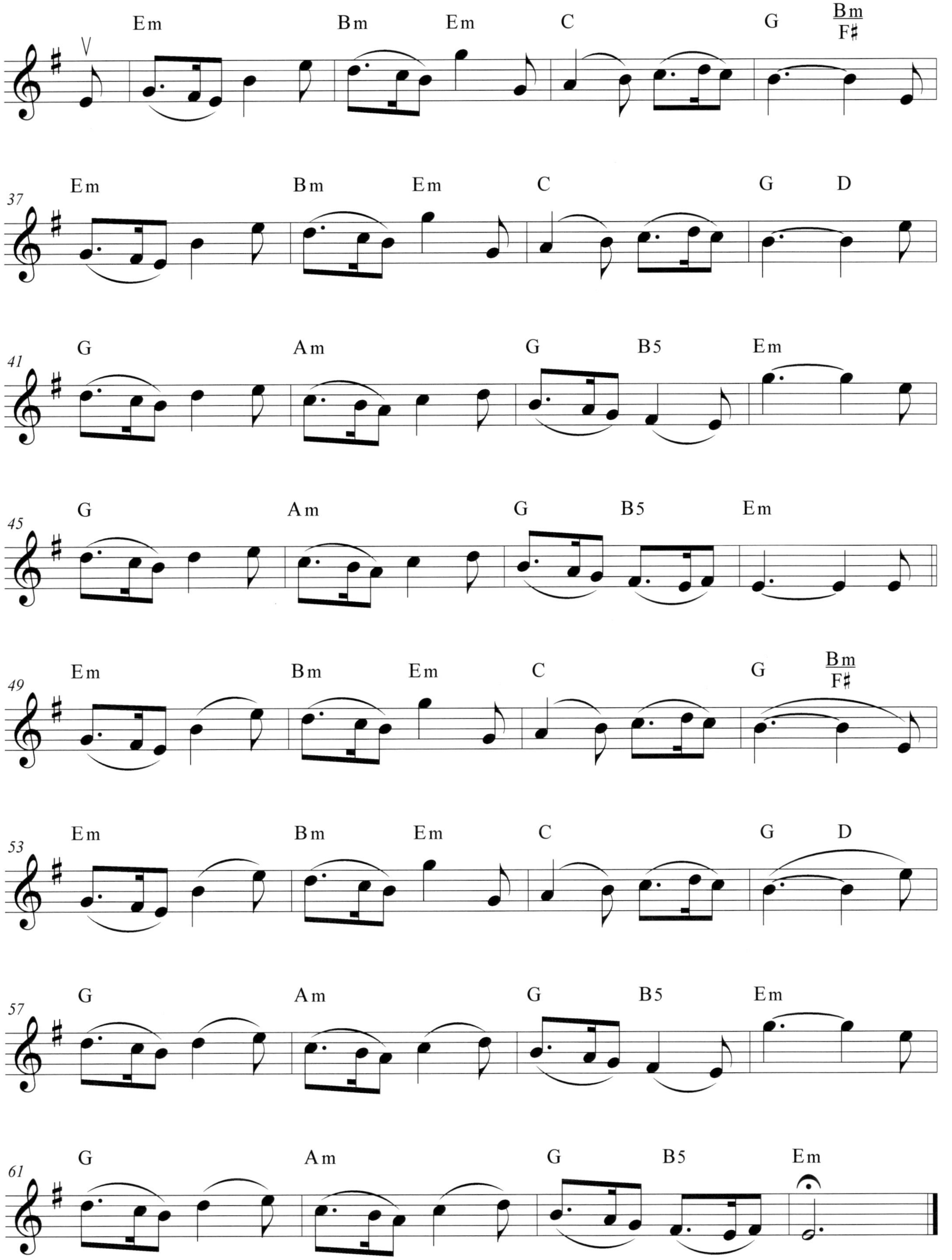

There are 4 variations of the tune presented here, 2 in Dm and 2 in Em. The chords changes are also different in three of the versions. Many interpretations work for the melodies in this book.

Fortune My Foe

♩ = 96--104

16th Century

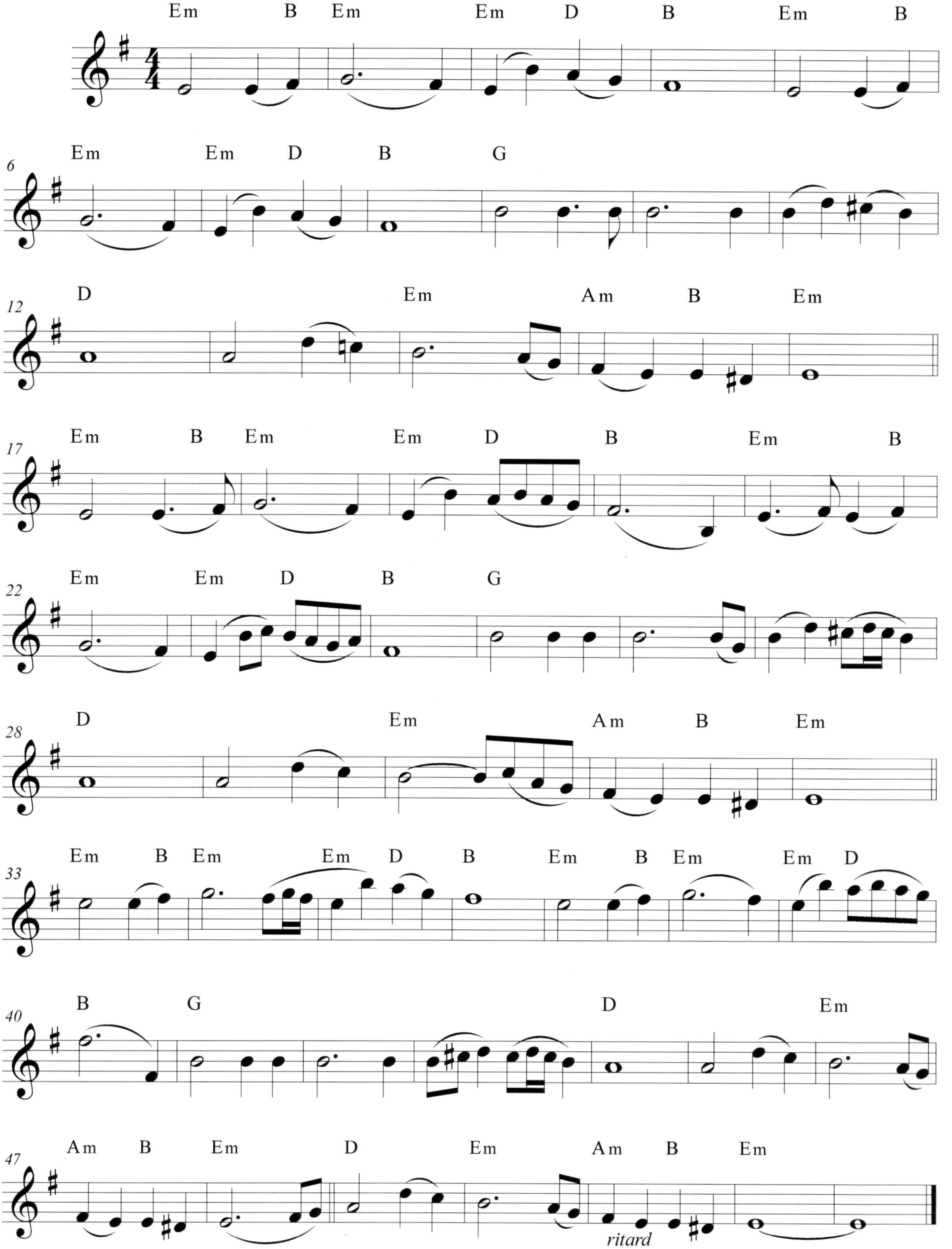

Greensleeves

Traditional English Ballad

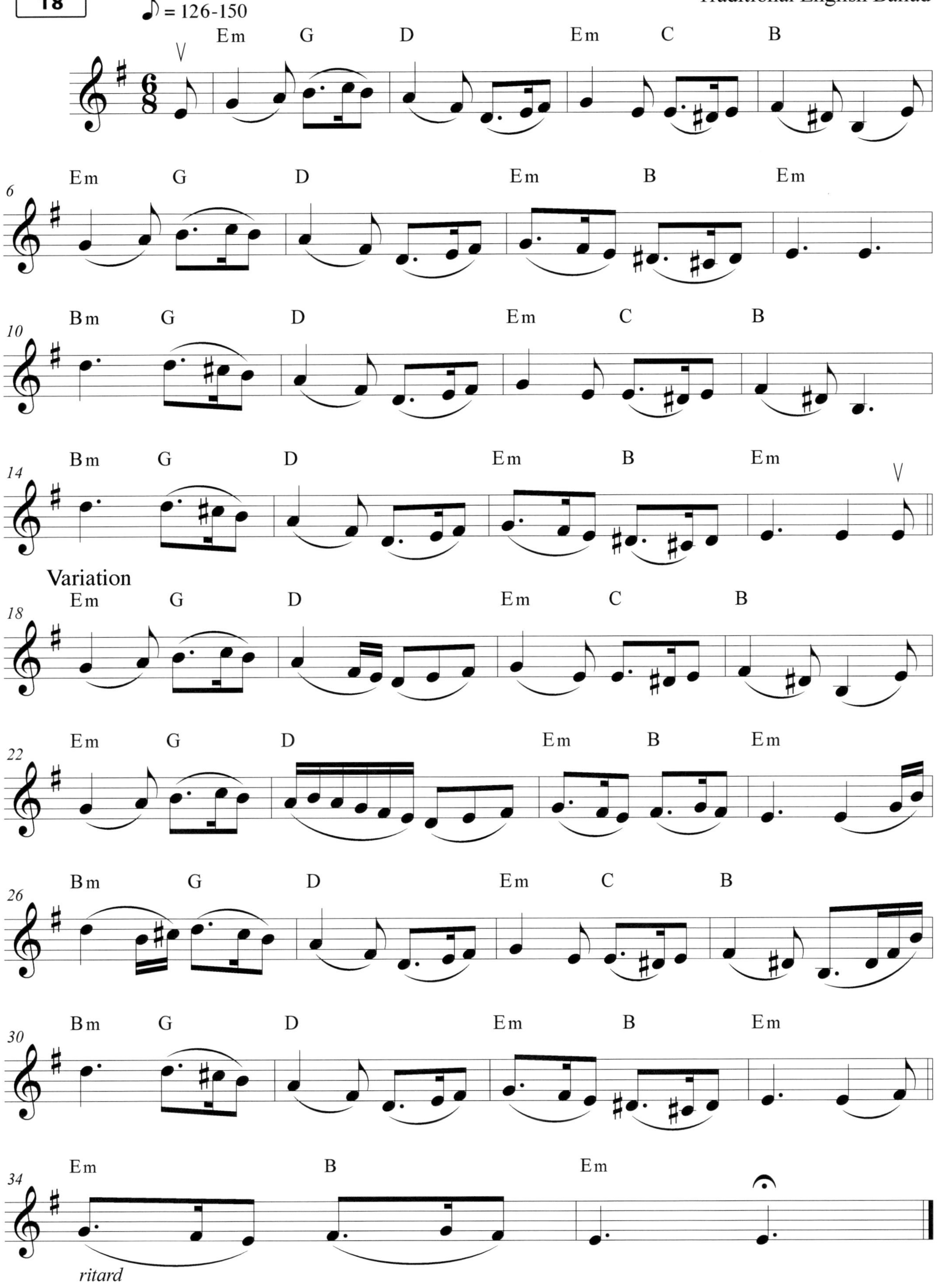

Grimstock

19

John Playford 1651

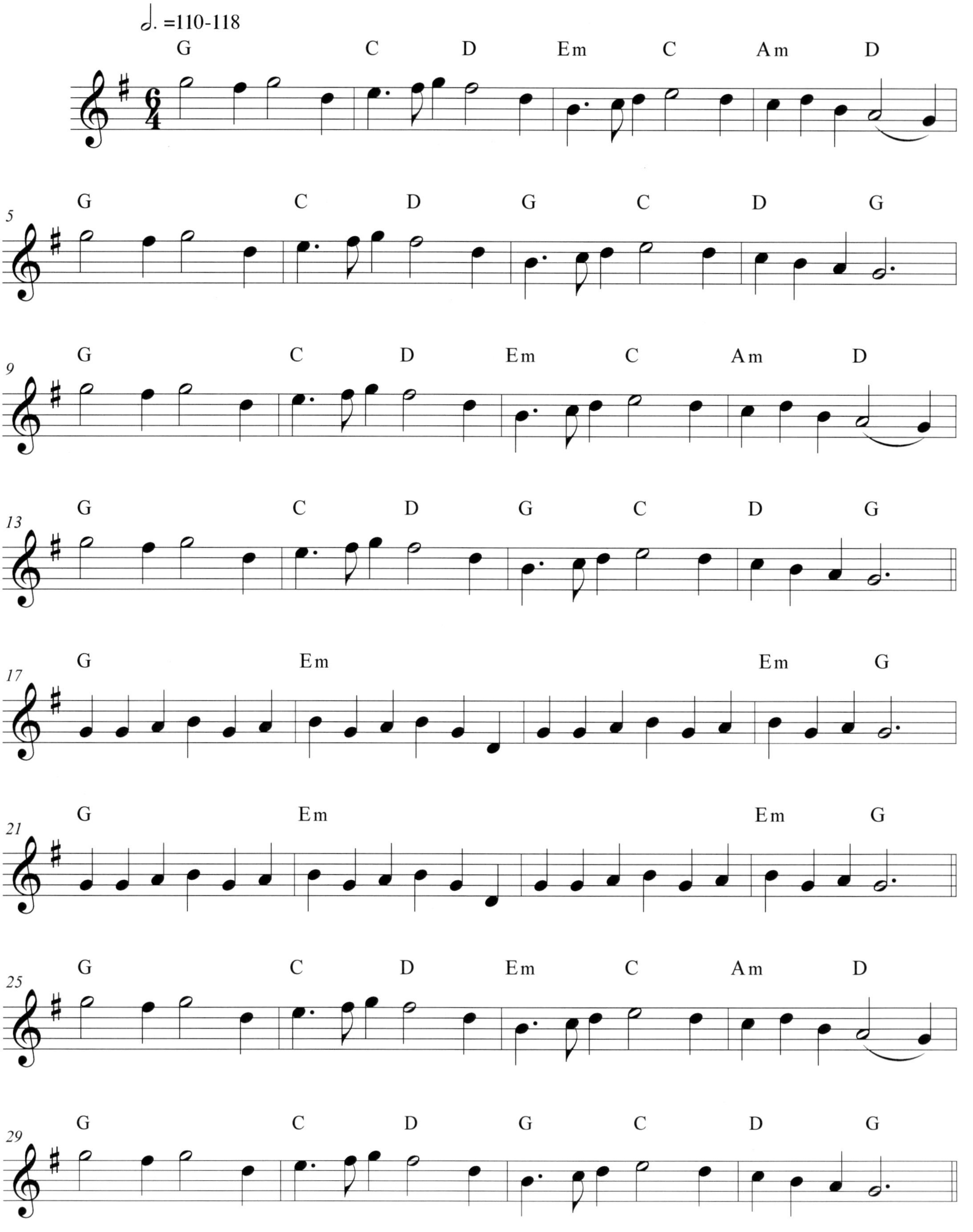

Alternate setting

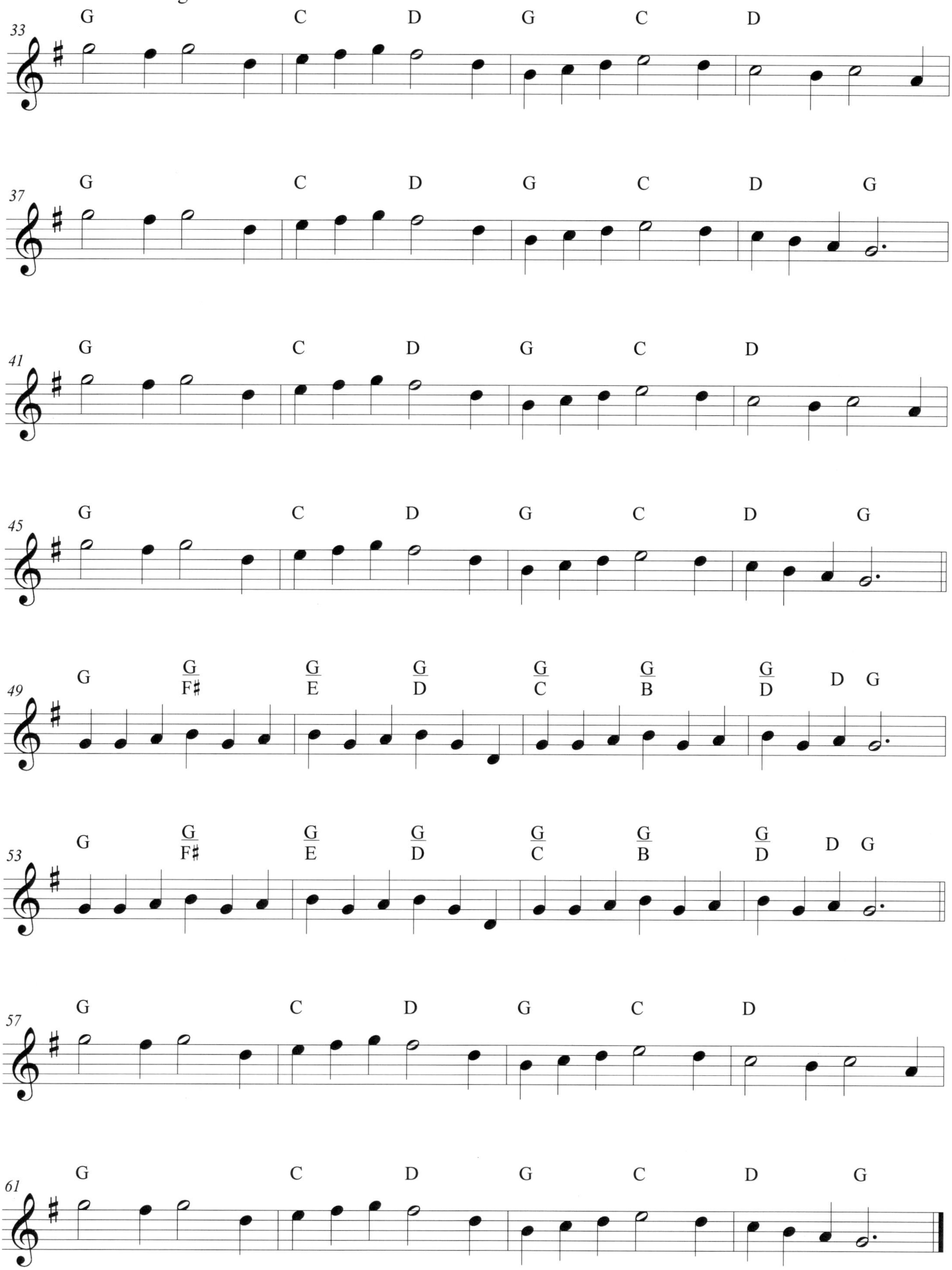

20

Harper's Frolic

Morris Dance

𝅗𝅥 = 96-106

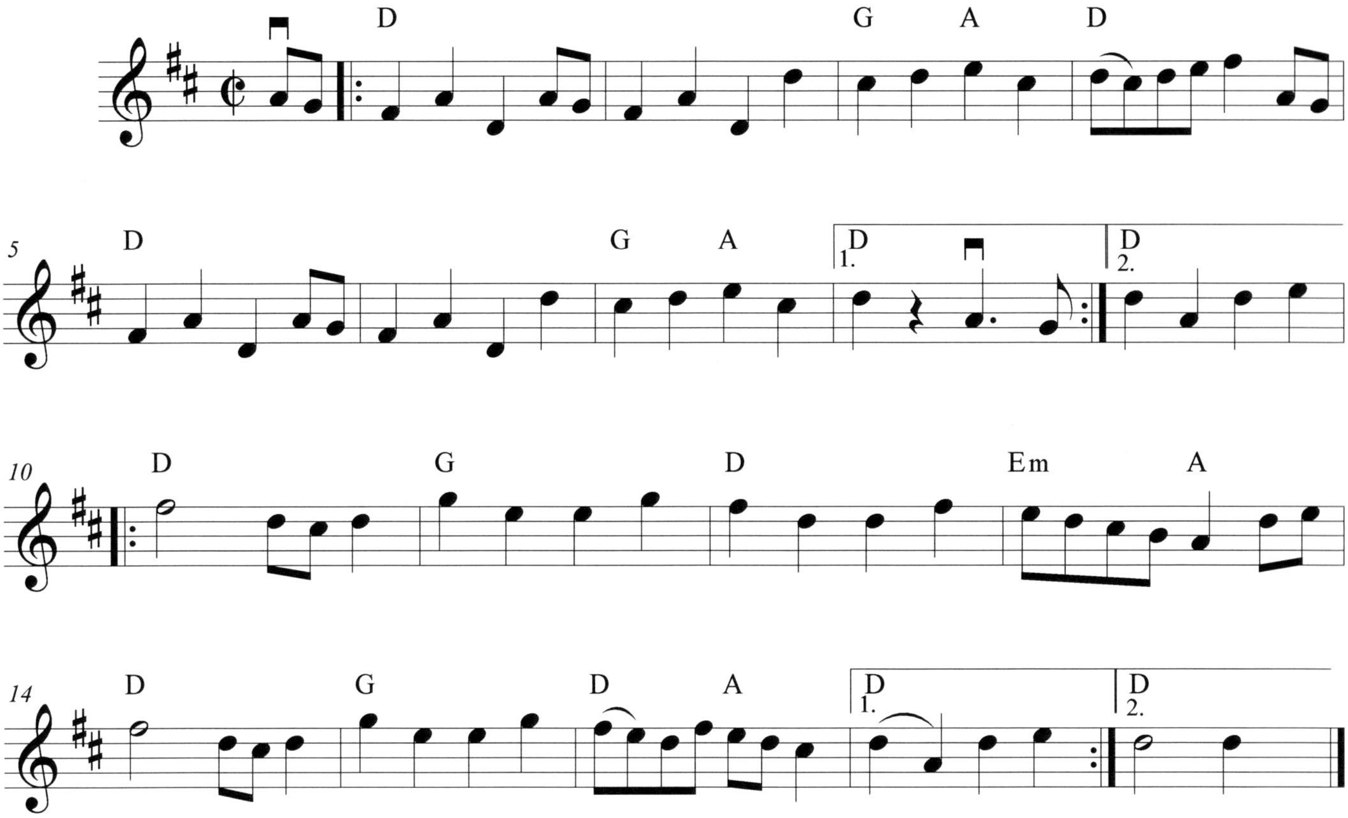

21

Bonny Kate

Morris Dance

𝅗𝅥 = 96-106

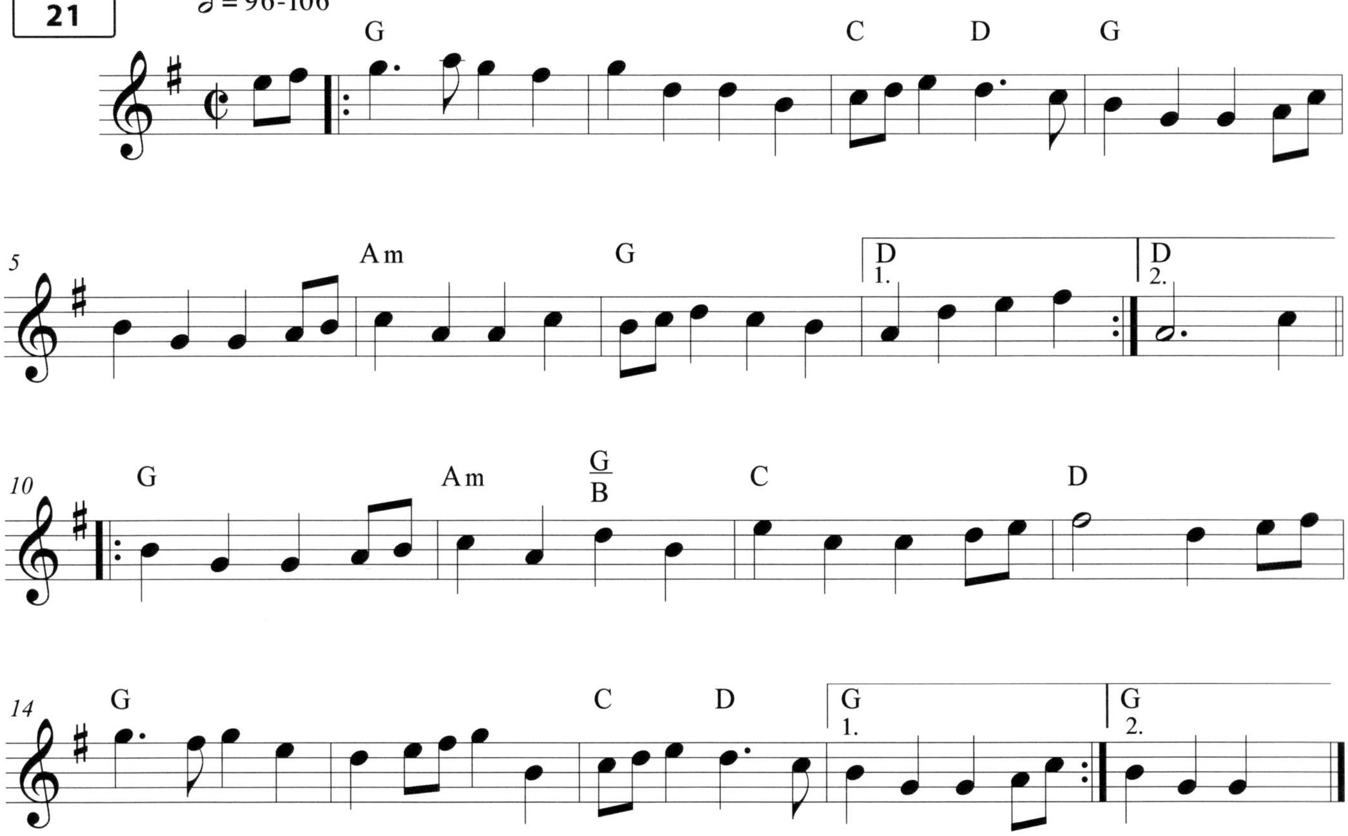

These tunes are often played together.

22

Heart's Ease

Misogonus c. 1560
John Playford 1651

♩. = 80-100

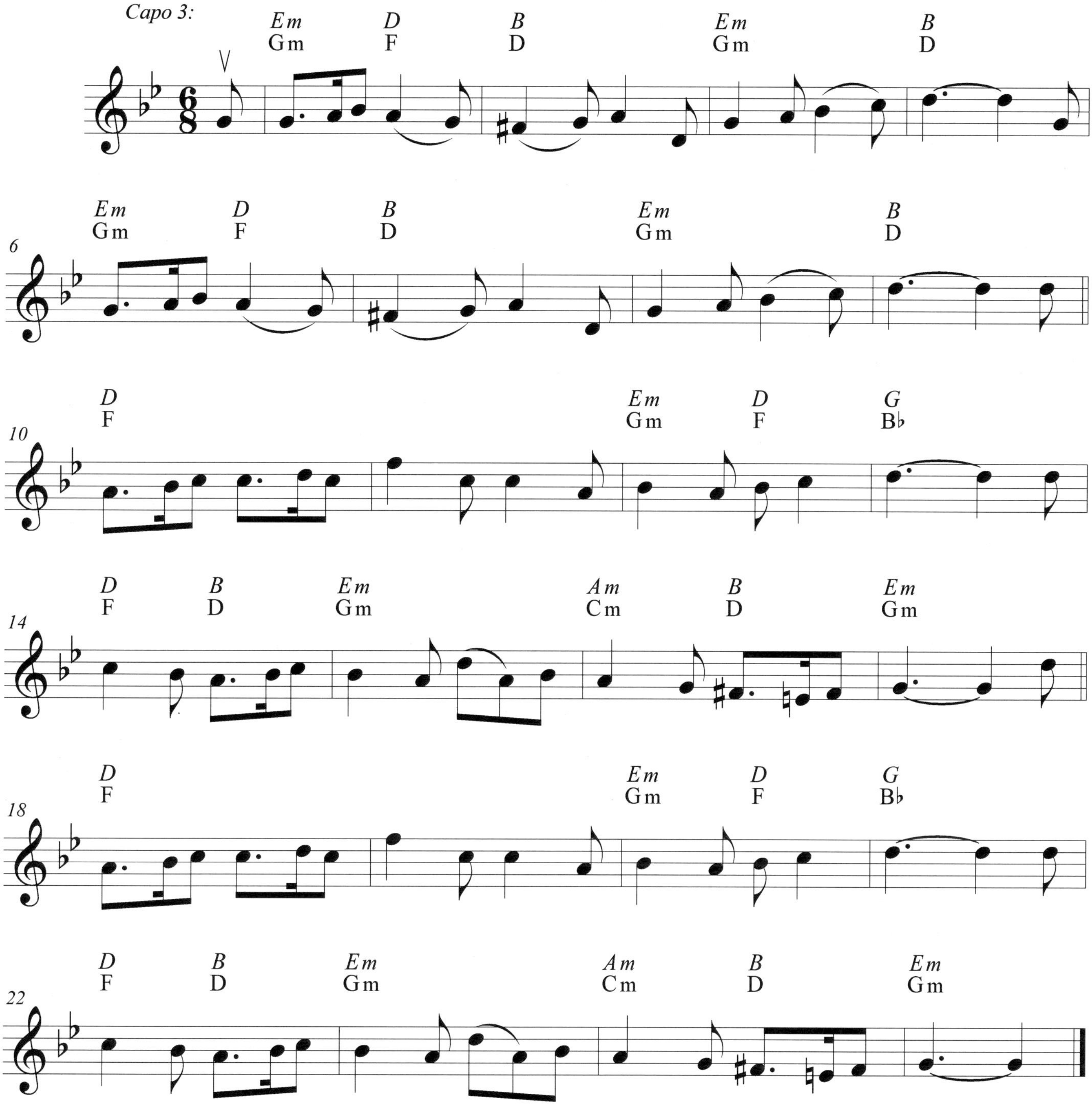

23

Helas madame

attributed to Henry VIII

𝅗𝅥 = 64-82

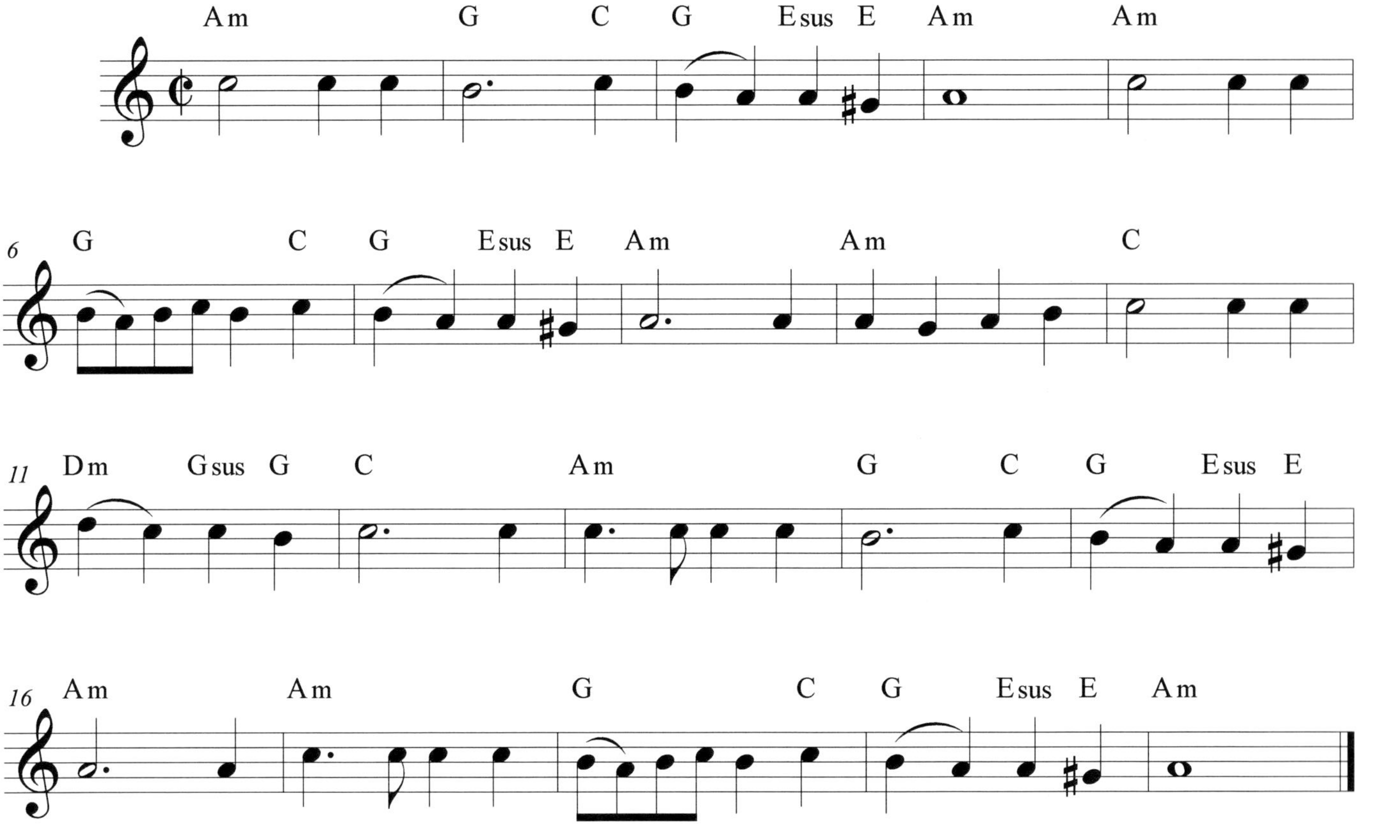

24

Highland Mary

Bampton

Morris Dance

𝅗𝅥 = 76-90

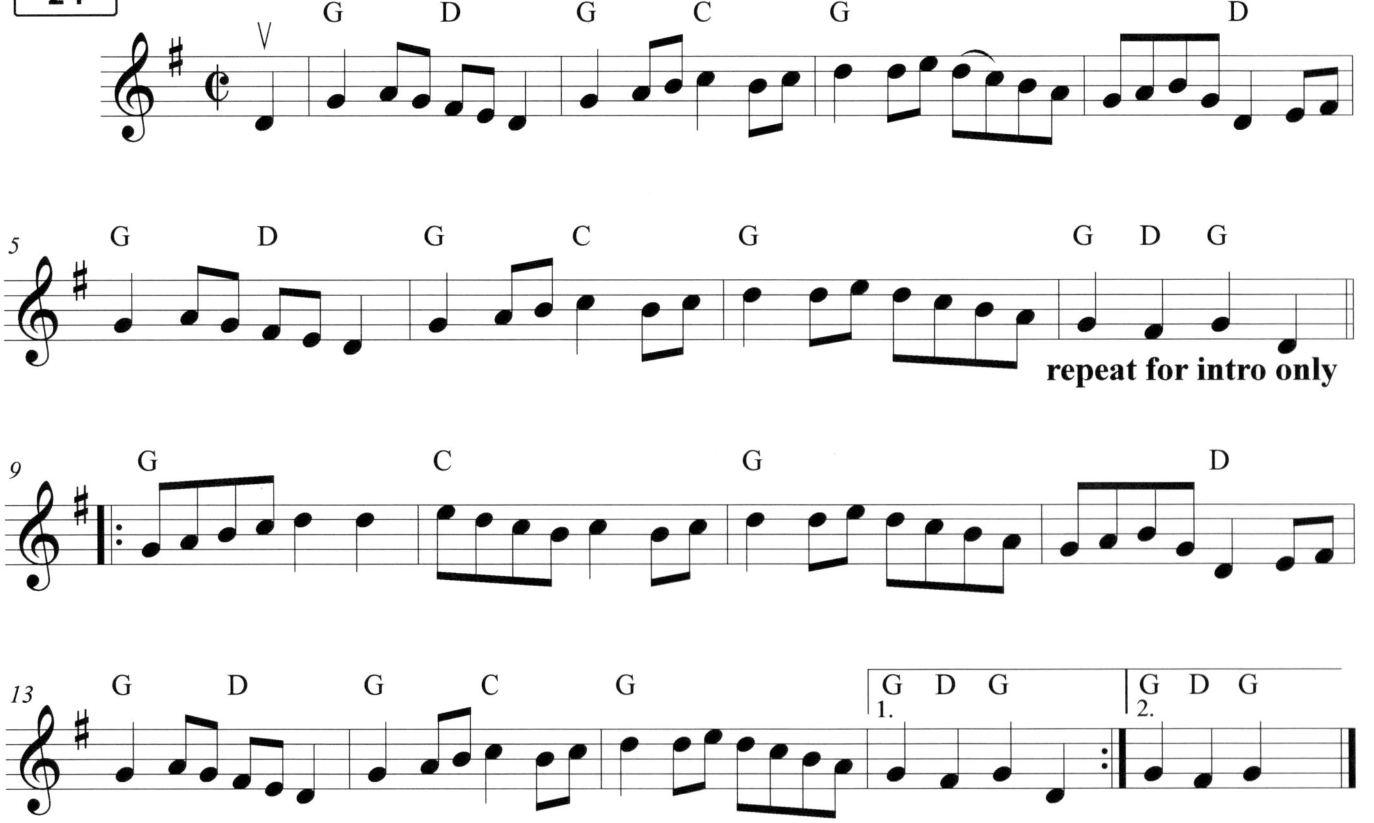

25

Hole in the Wall

Henry Purcell (1659-1695)

♩ = 76-80

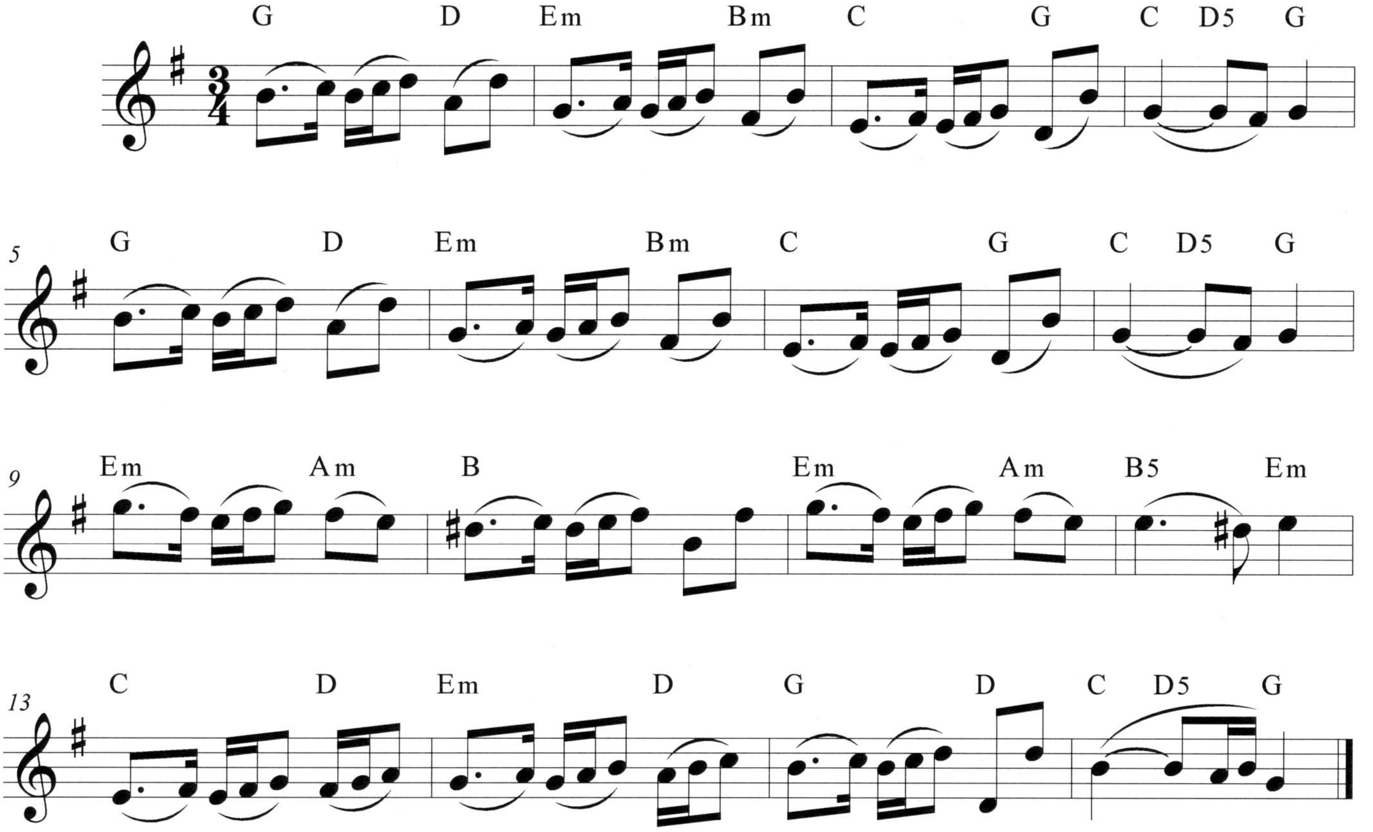

26

Hunsdon House

John Playford 1670

♩. = 82-98

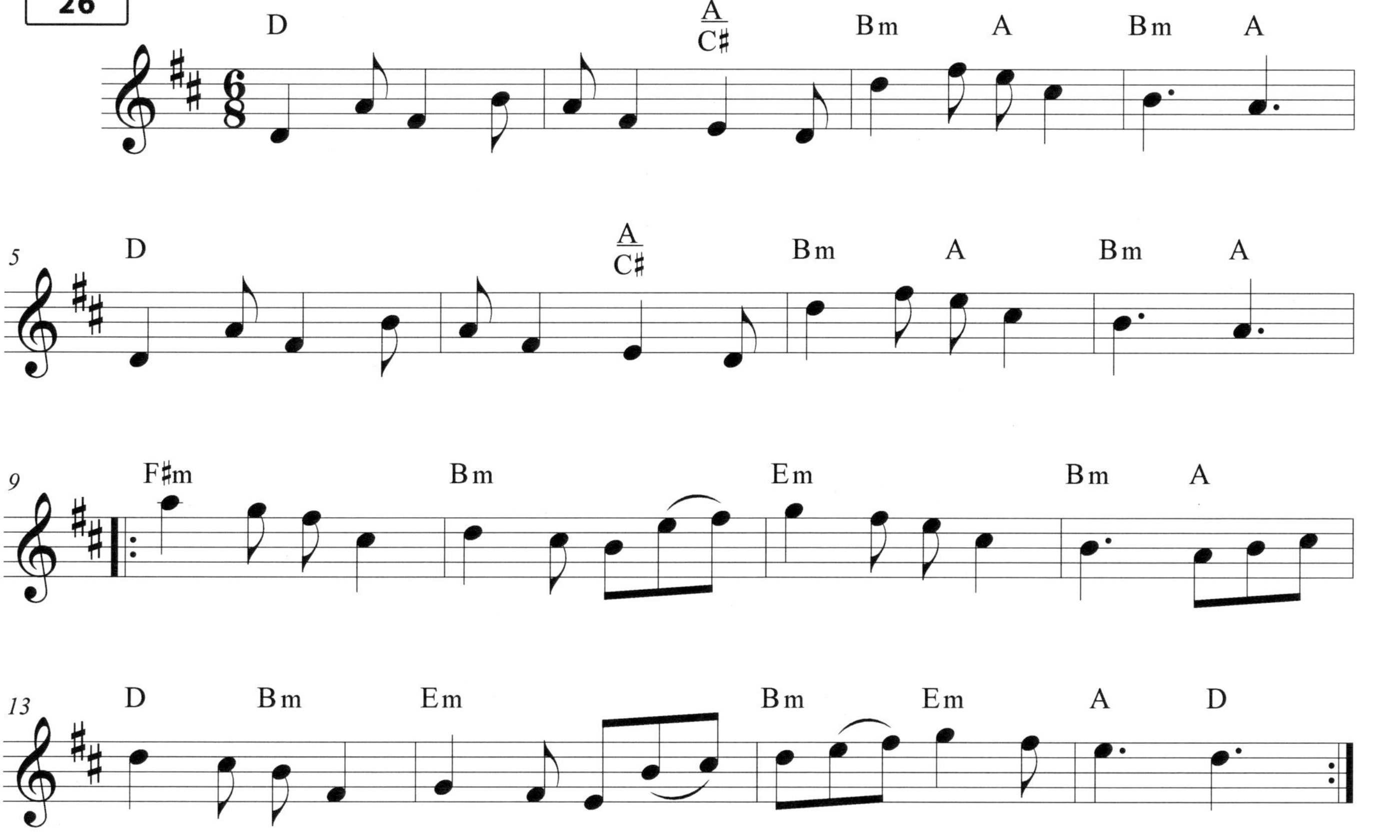

27

Jamaica

Jameko

John Playford 1670

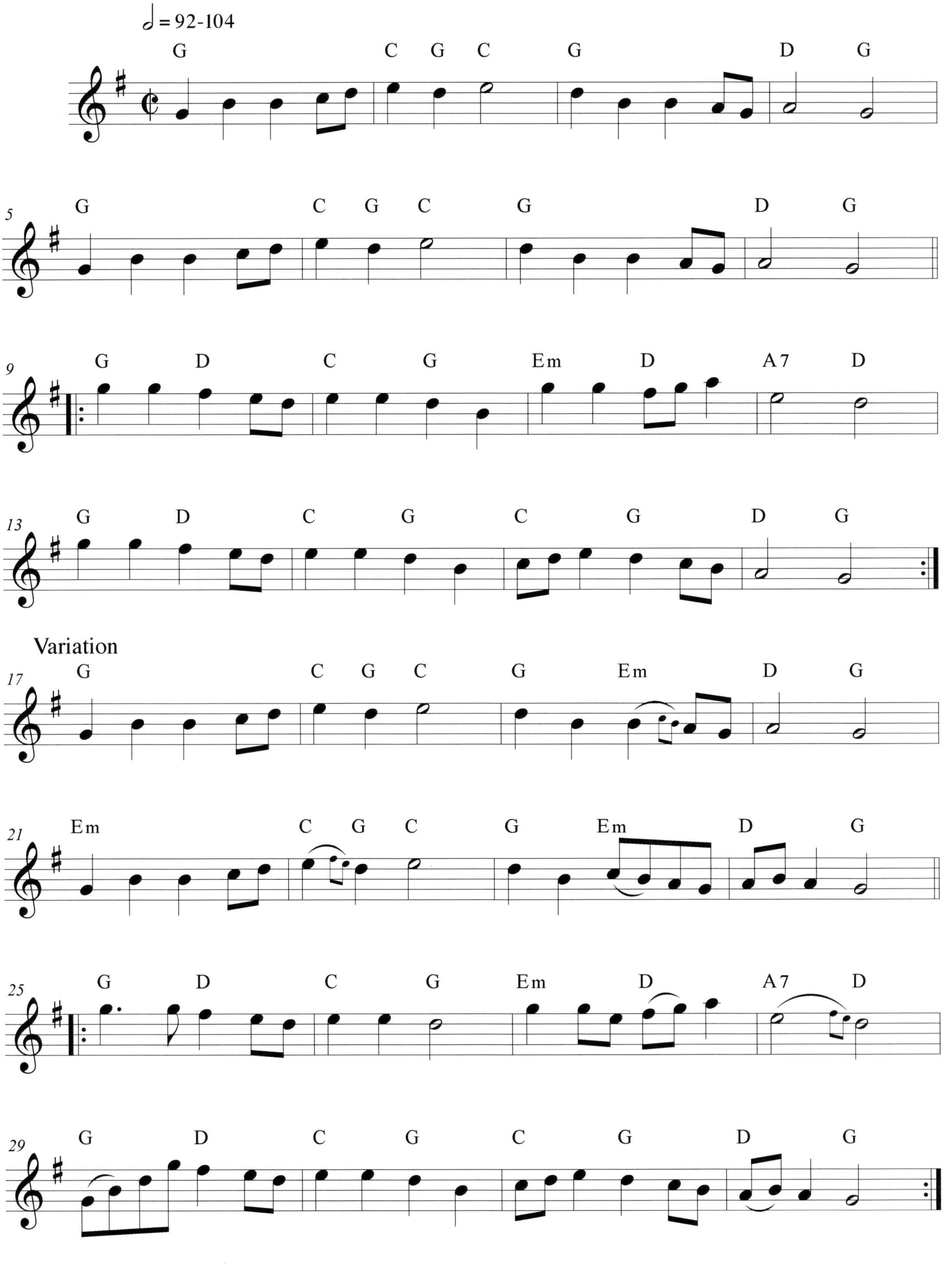

28

Kemp's Jig

𝅗𝅥 = 92-102

English Country Dance 17th Century

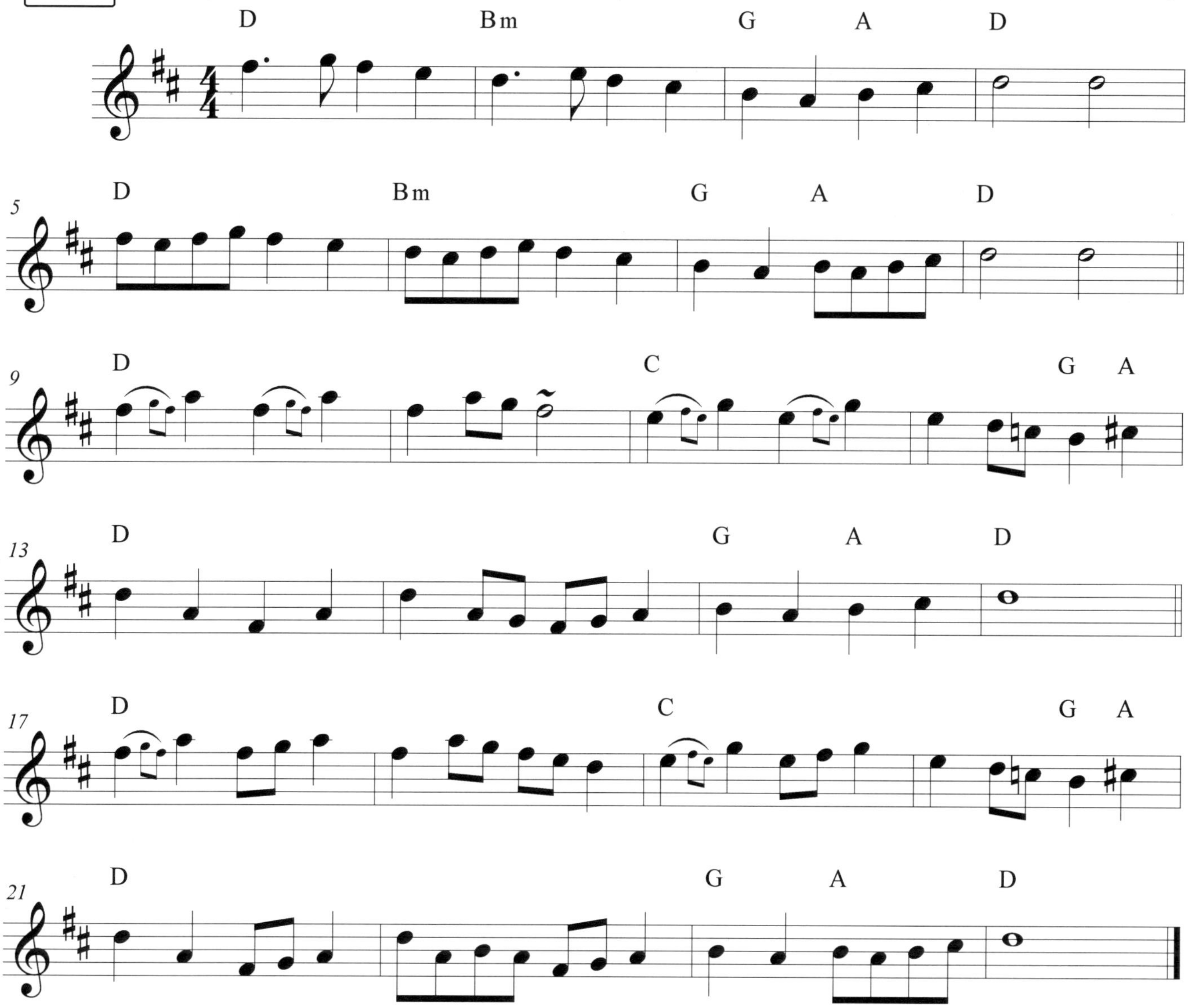

29

Kemp's Jig

♩. = 68-76

John Playford 1651

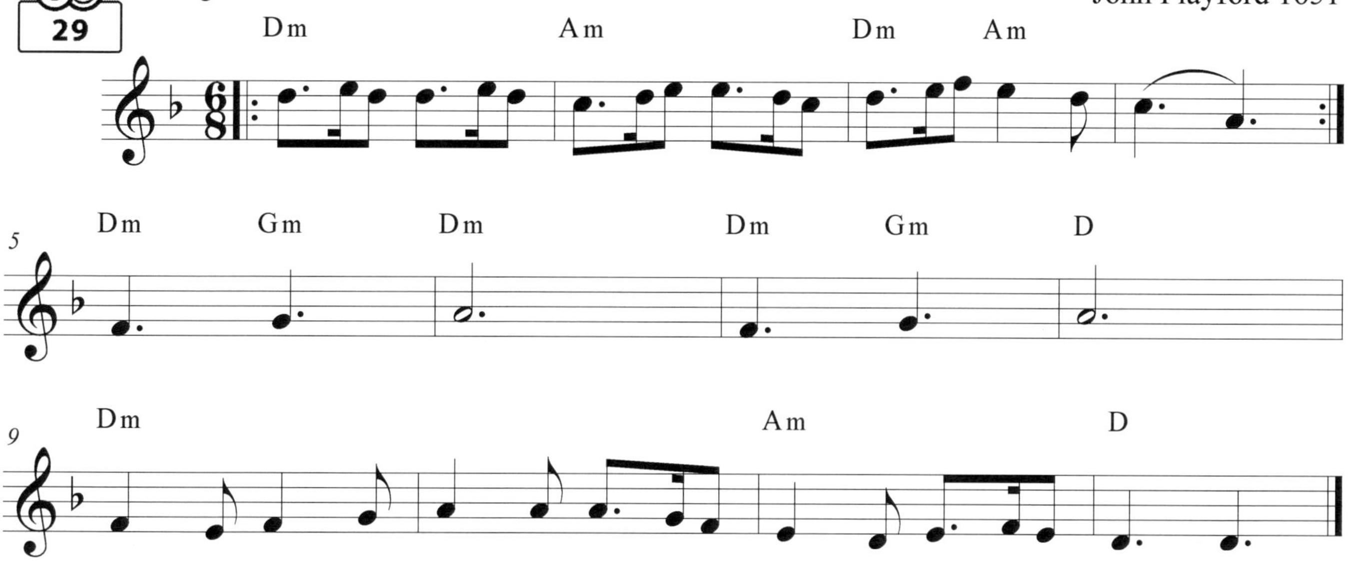

30

Juice of Barley
Cold and Raw the North Wind Doth Blow

both titles appear in The Dancing Master
John Playford 1651-1728

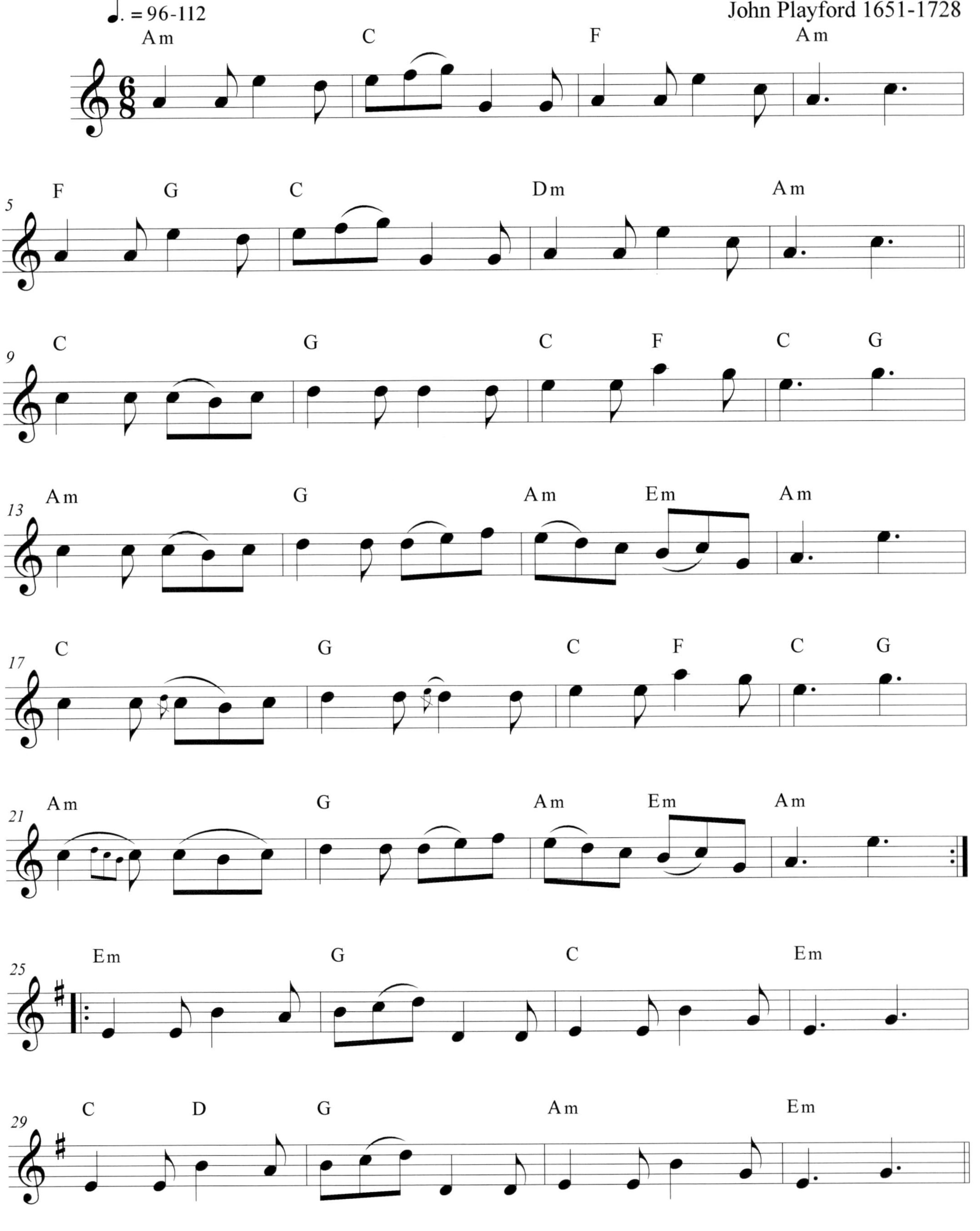

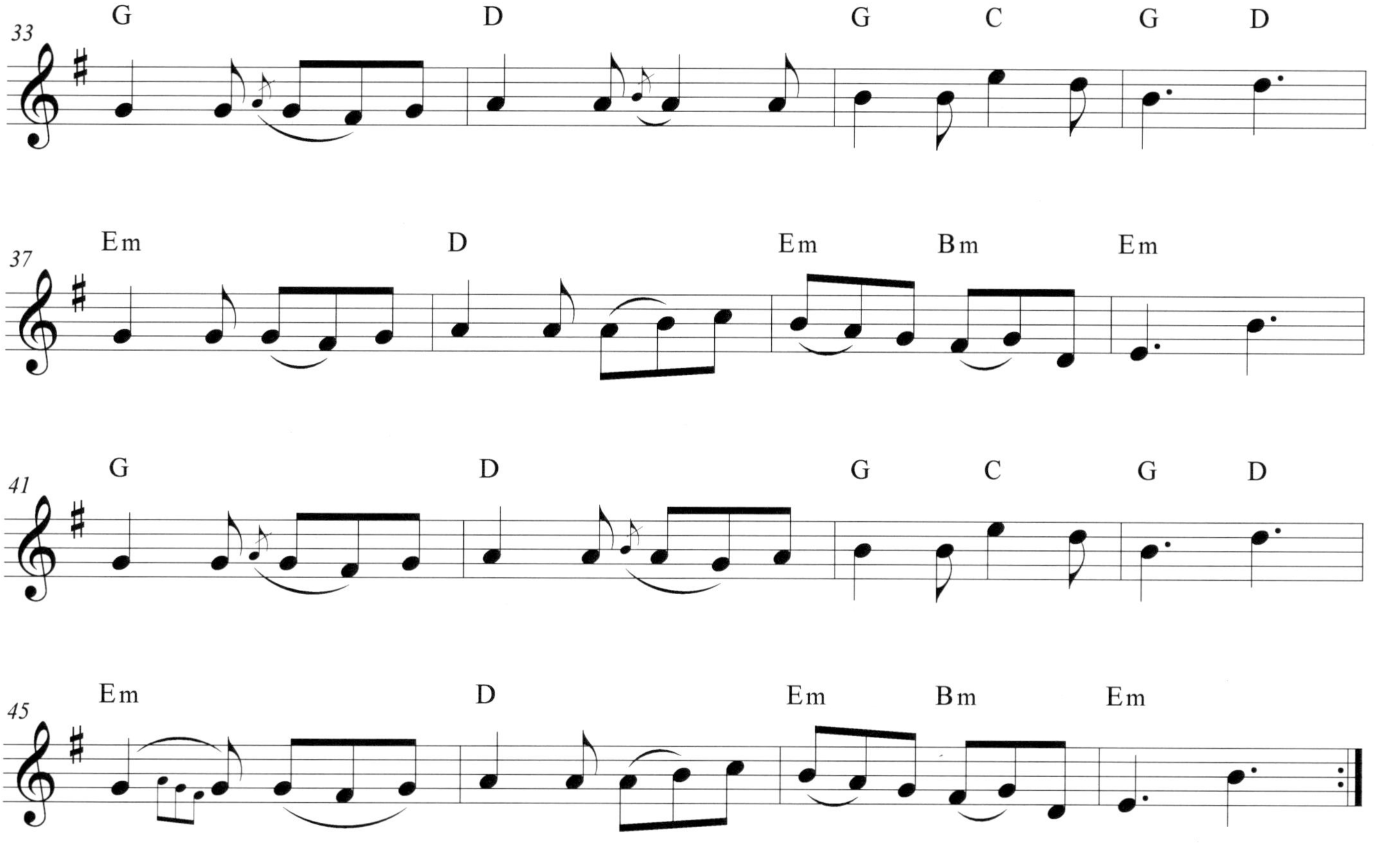

Lilliburlero

♩. = 94-106

First published in London 1661

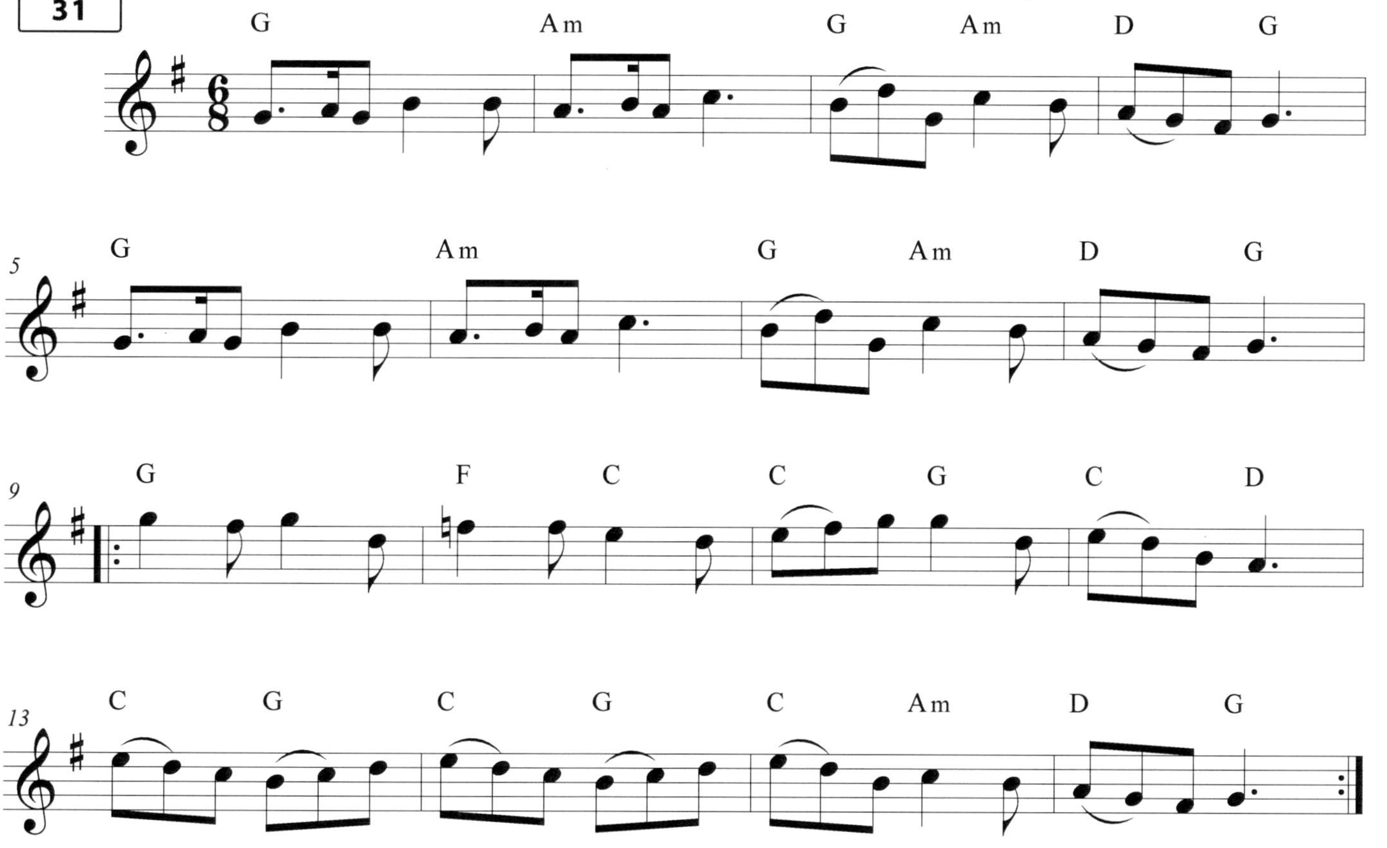

32

Man in the Moon

Traditional English Waltz

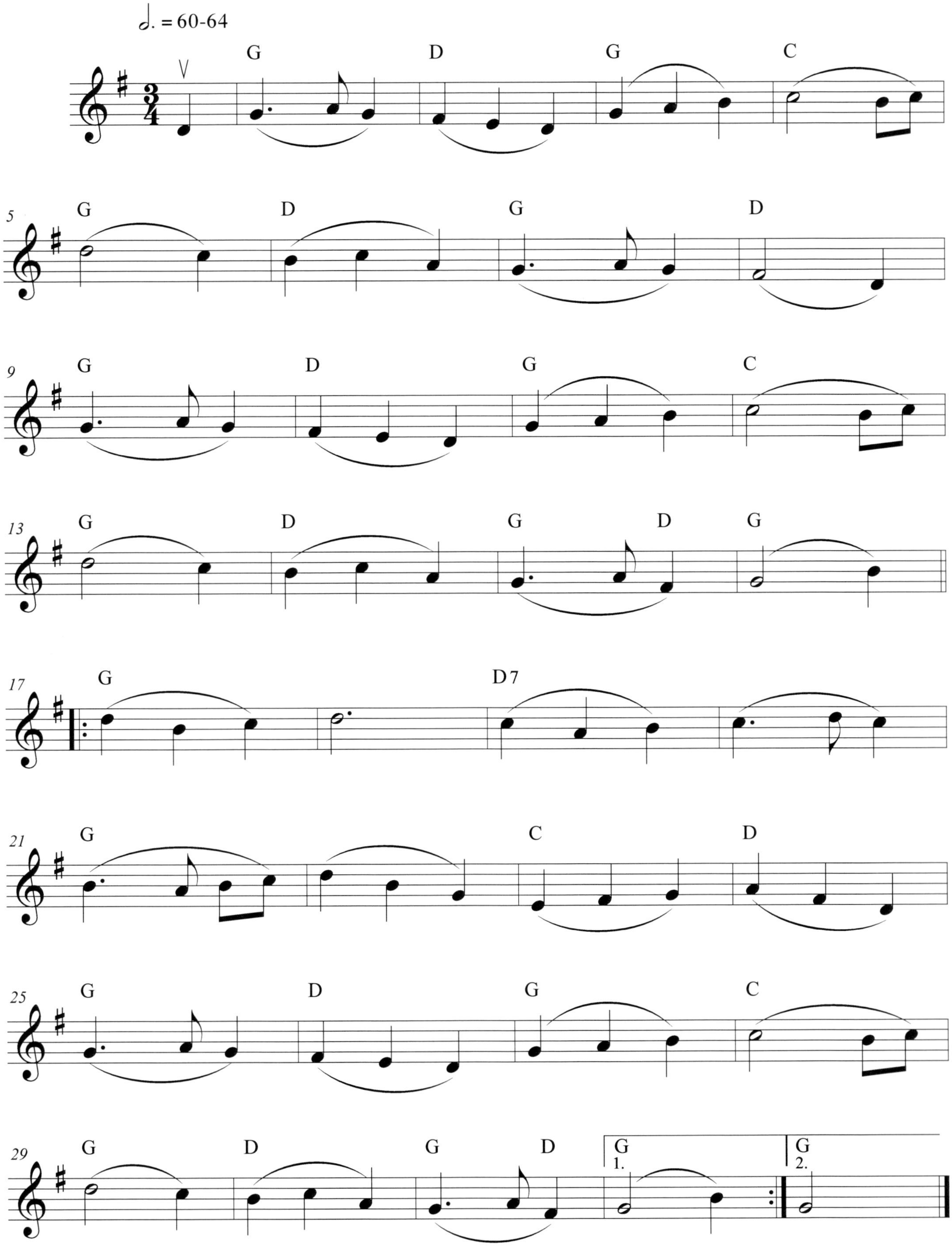

33

Newcastle

𝅗𝅥 = 92-112

John Playford 1651

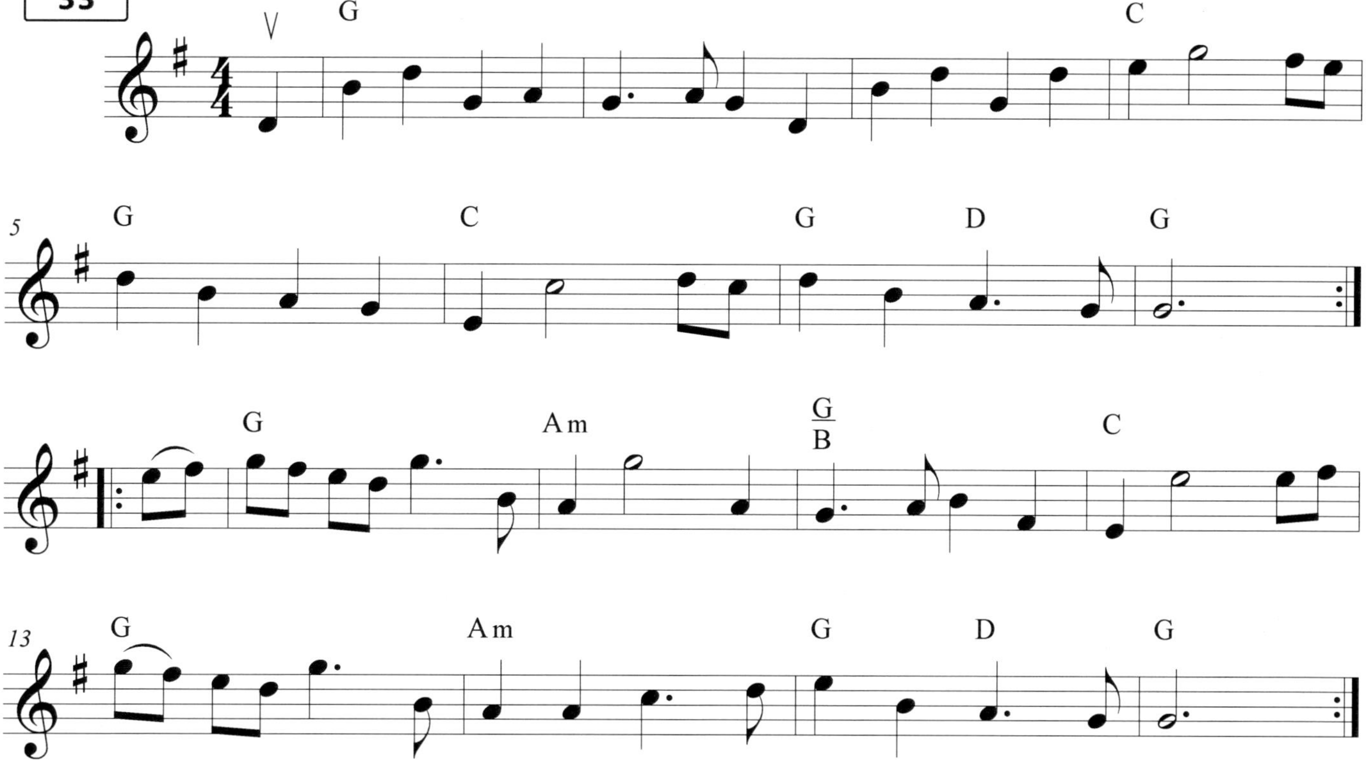

34

Packington's Pound

𝅘𝅥𝅮 = 136-148

16th Century English

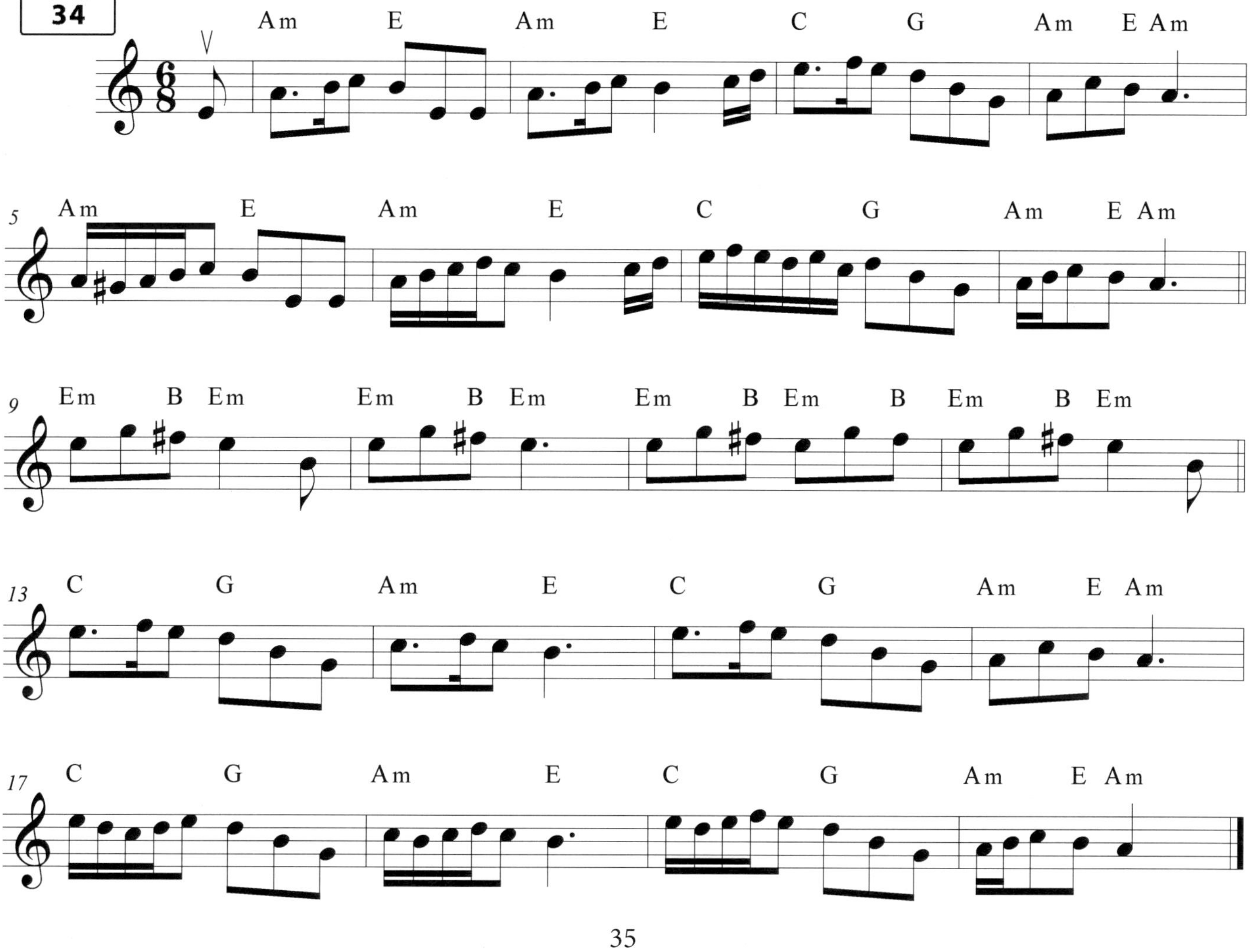

35

Off She Goes

English Country Dance

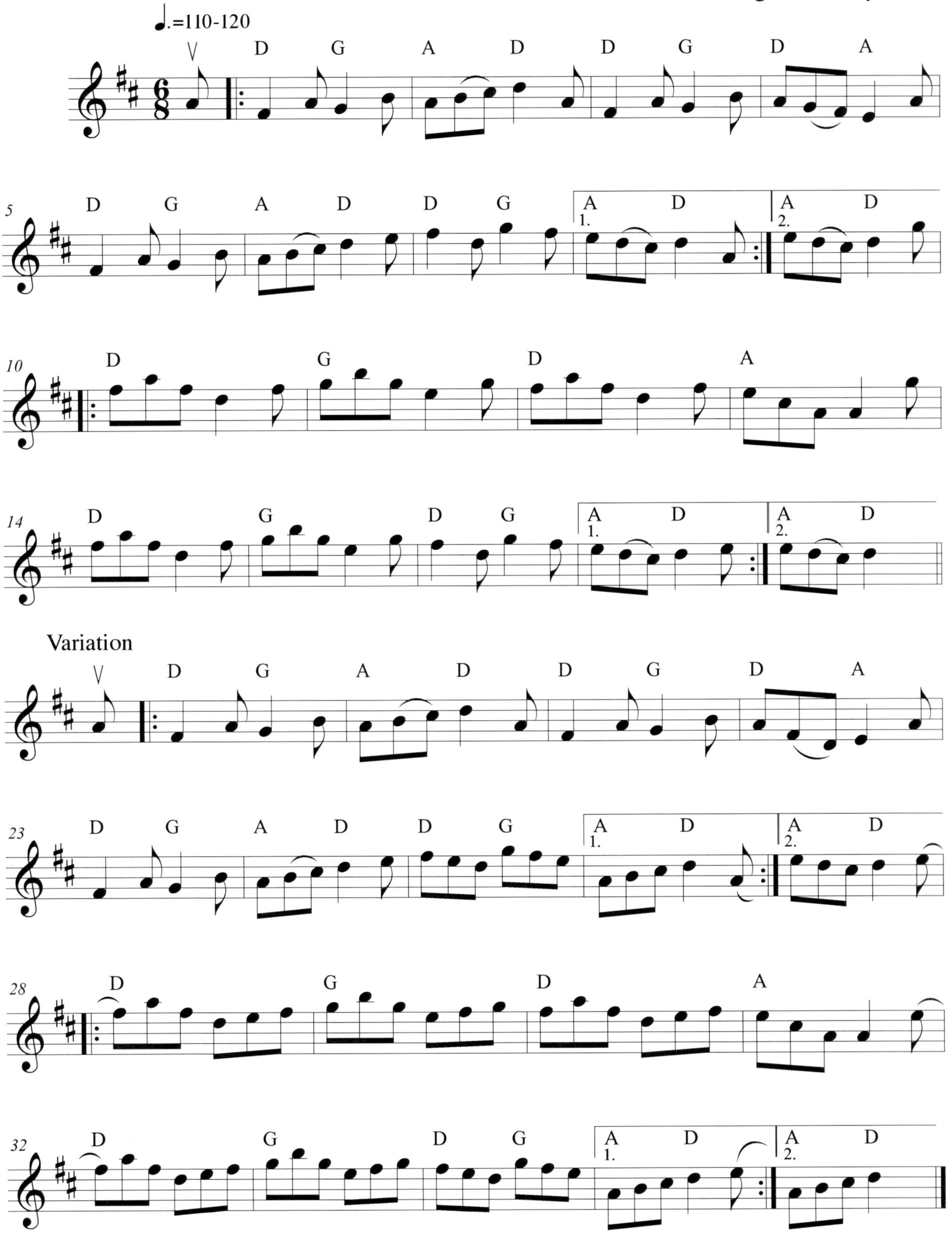

36

The Old Bachelor

Wells Humour

Henry Purcell 1691

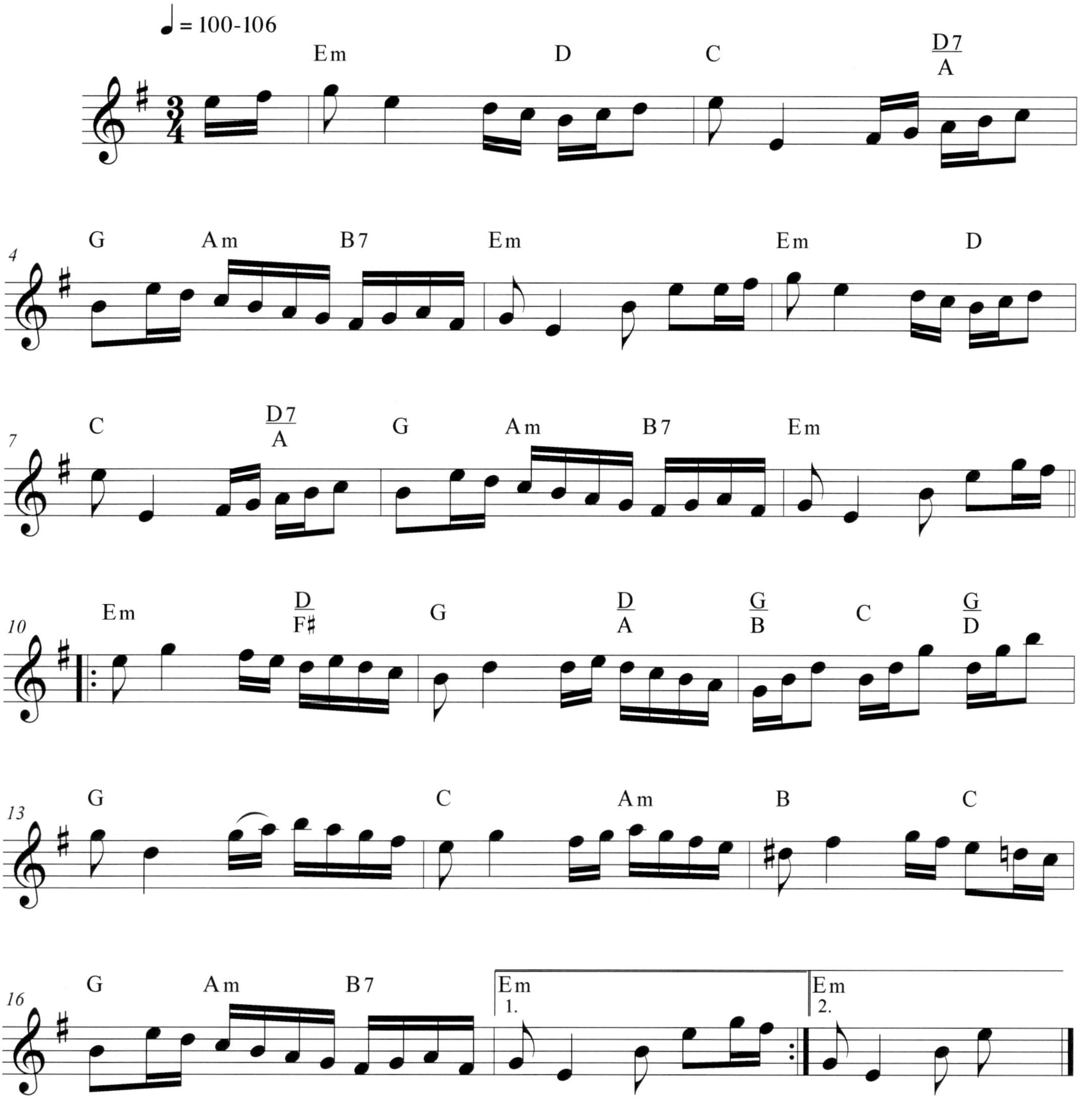

37

Parson's Farewell

John Playford 1651

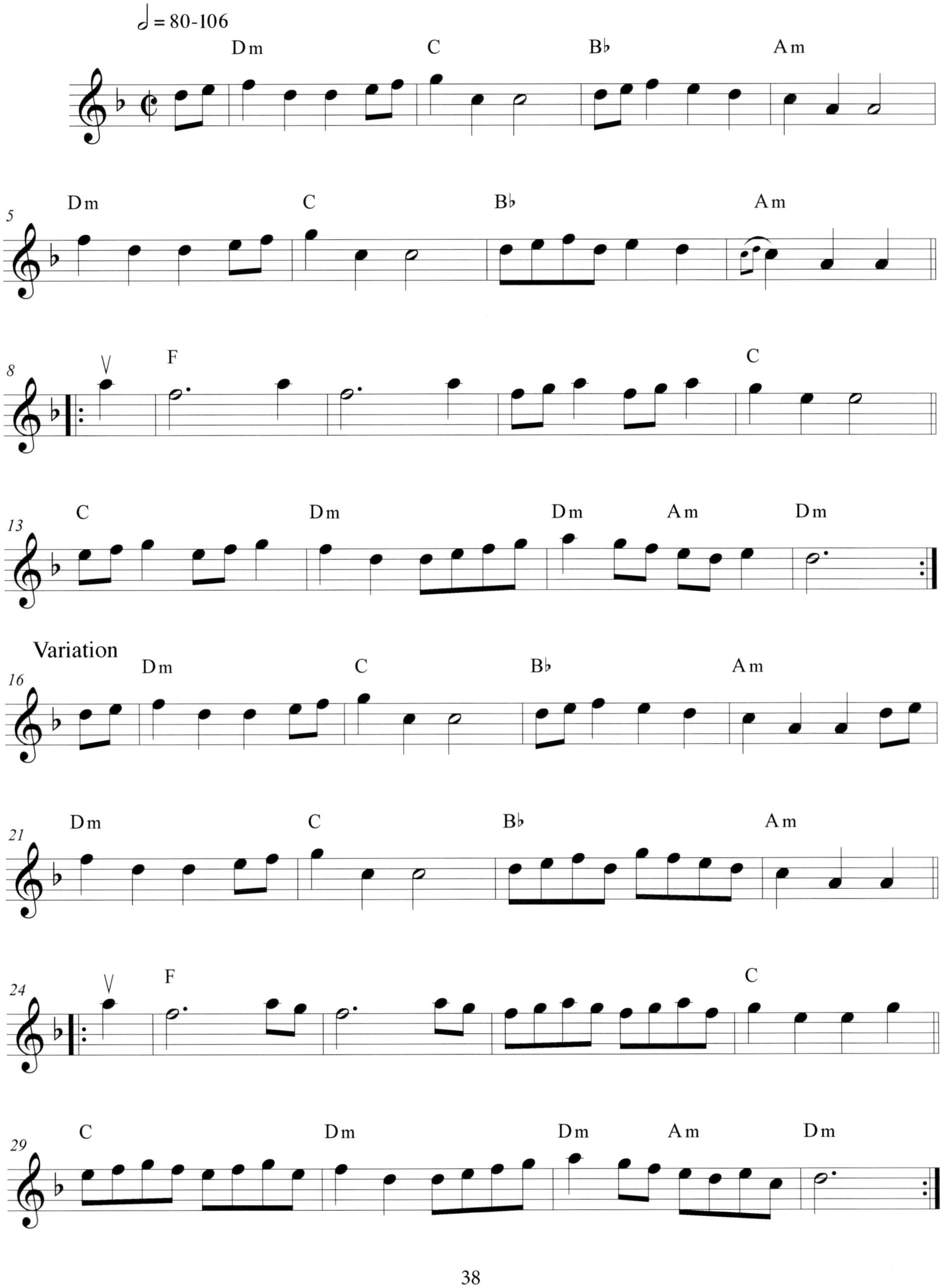

38

Portsmouth

John Playford 1701

𝅗𝅥 = 96-112

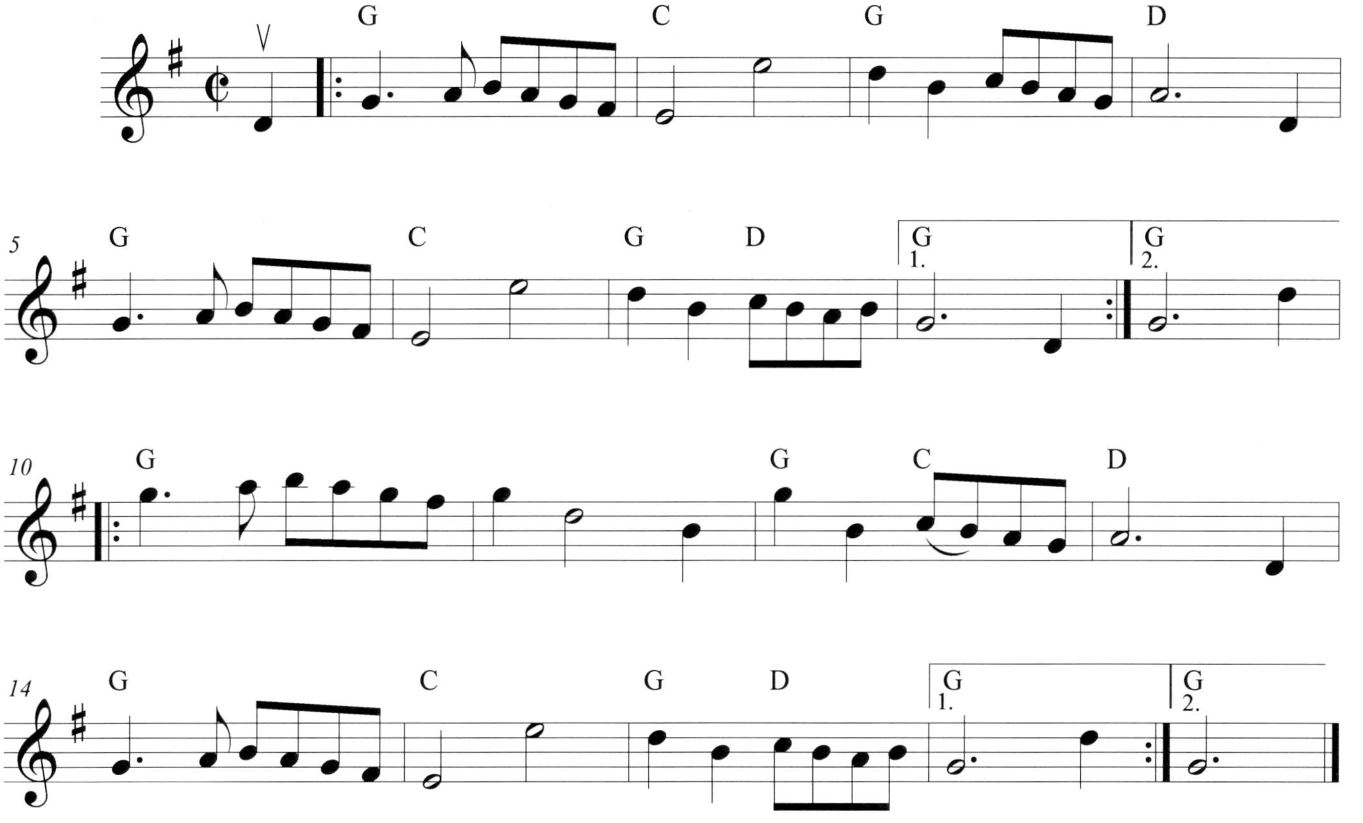

39

Staines Morris

Traditional English

𝅗𝅥 = 64-84

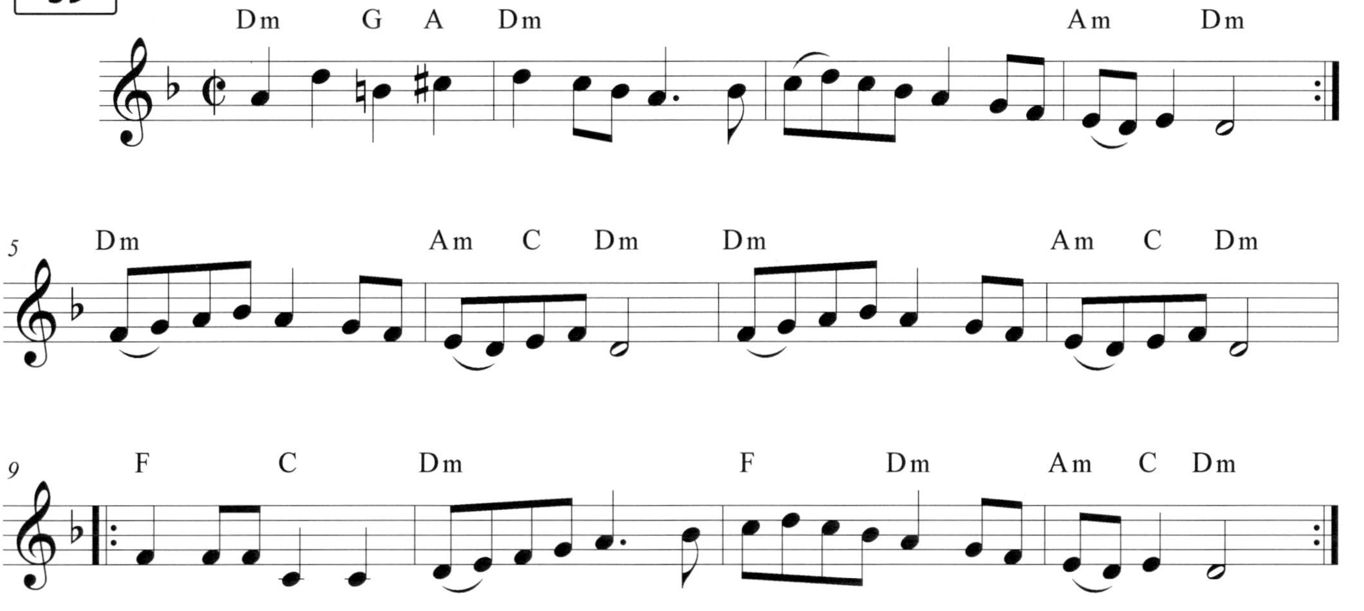

Note: Vocal versions of the song do not repeat the first 4 measures, but most instrumental versions do.

Prince Rupert's March

John Playford 1651

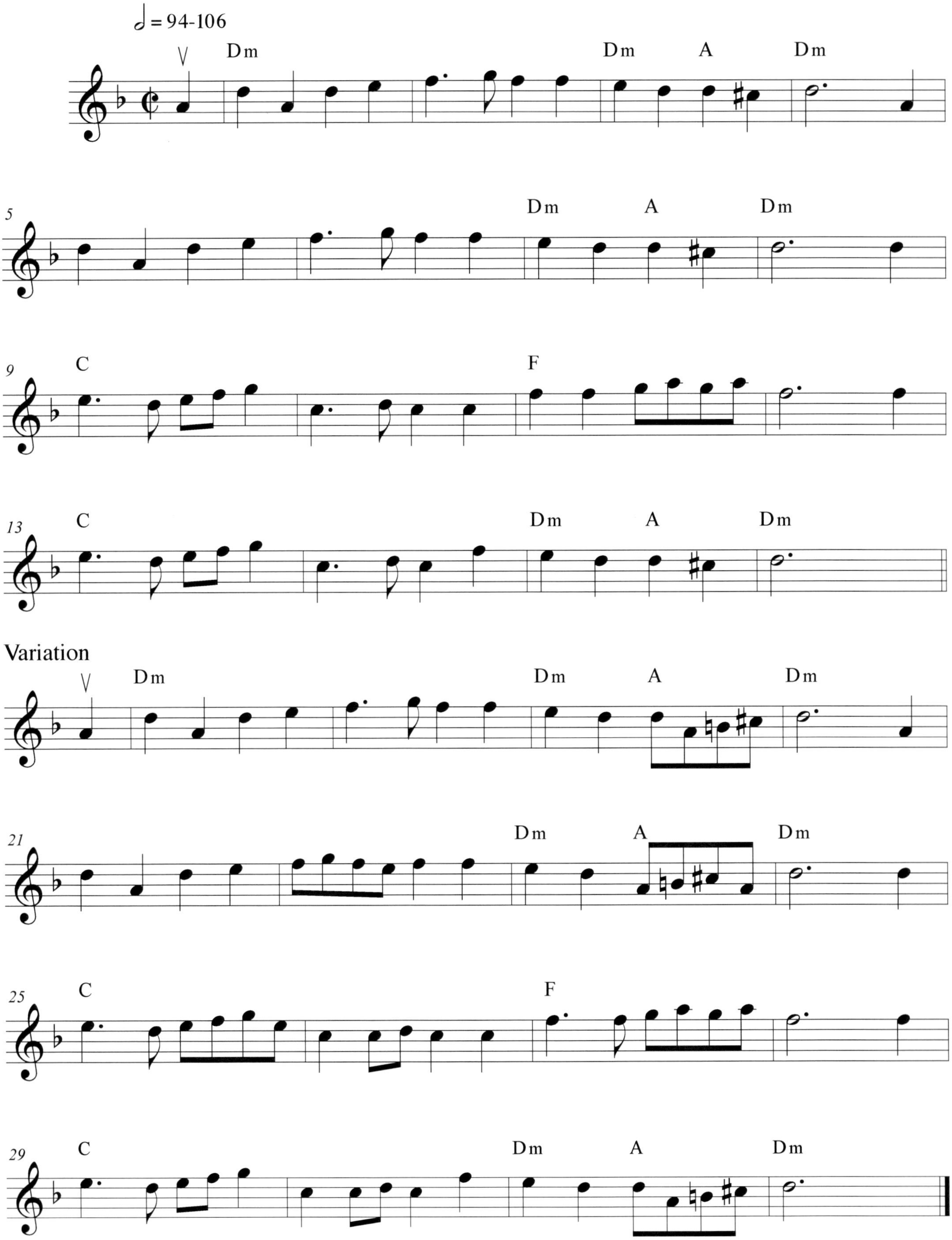

41

The Cutty Wren
Rafe's Waltz

Traditional English

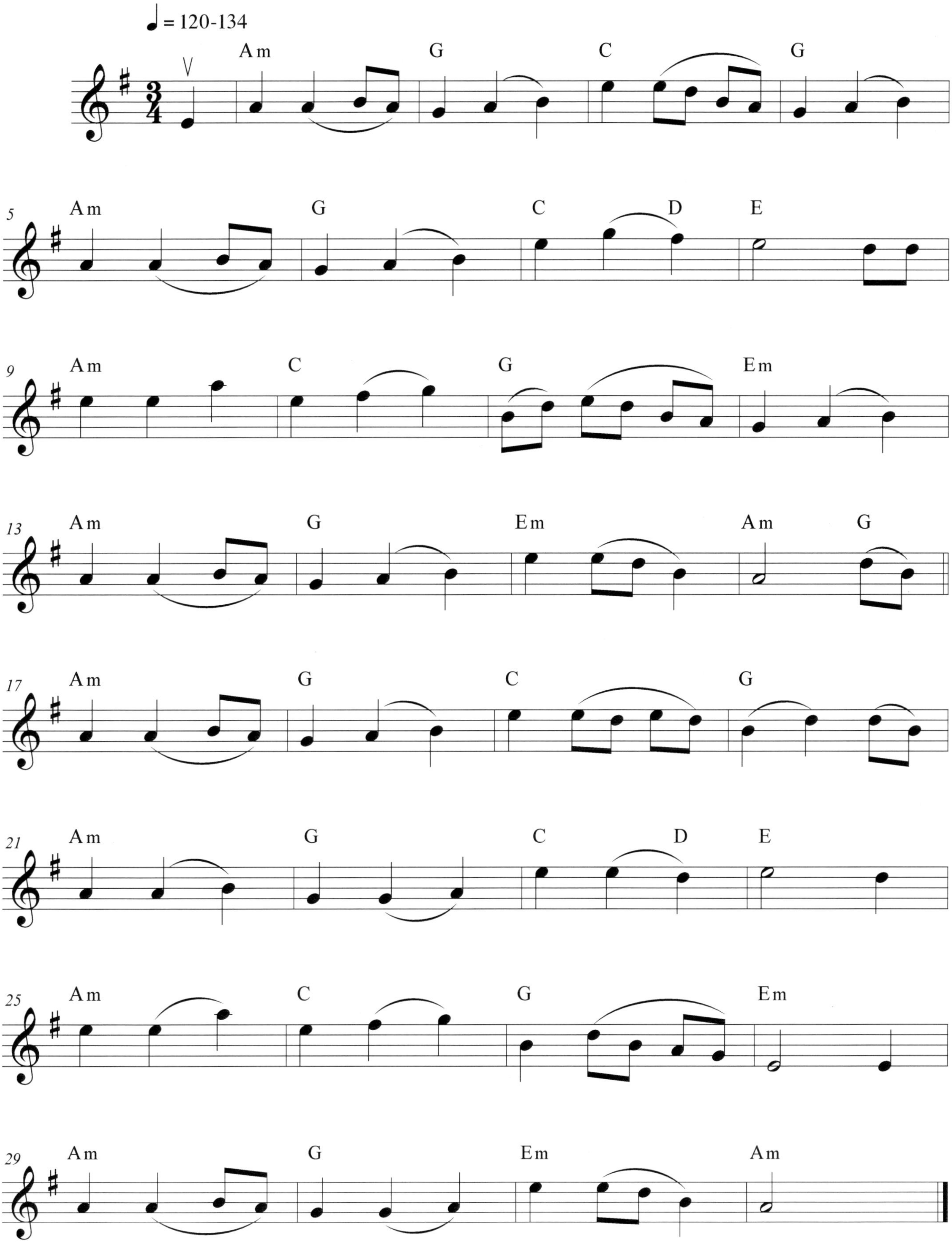

42

Salterello

Italiana

Guitar: Dropped-D Tuning

Vincenzo Galilei (1520-1591)

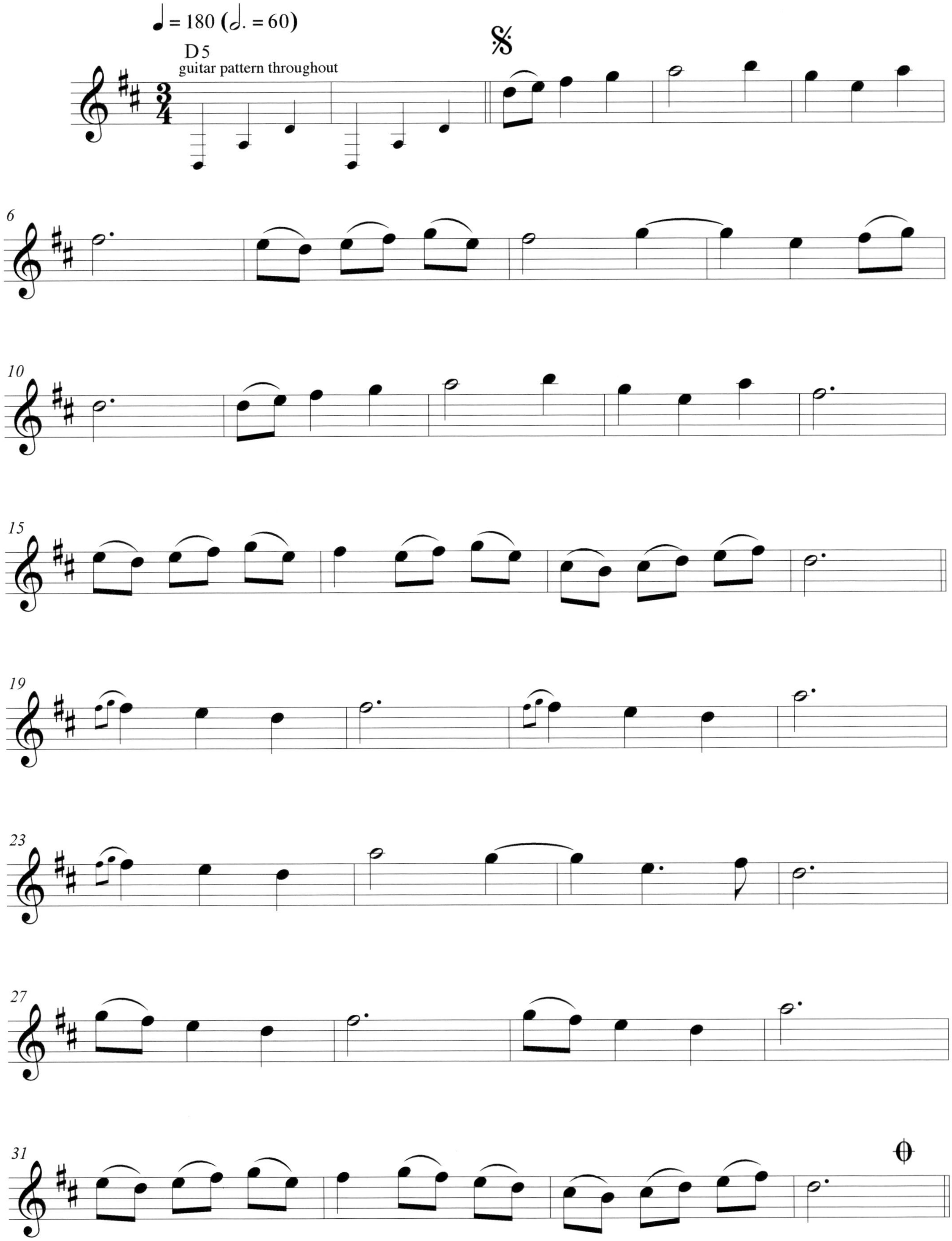

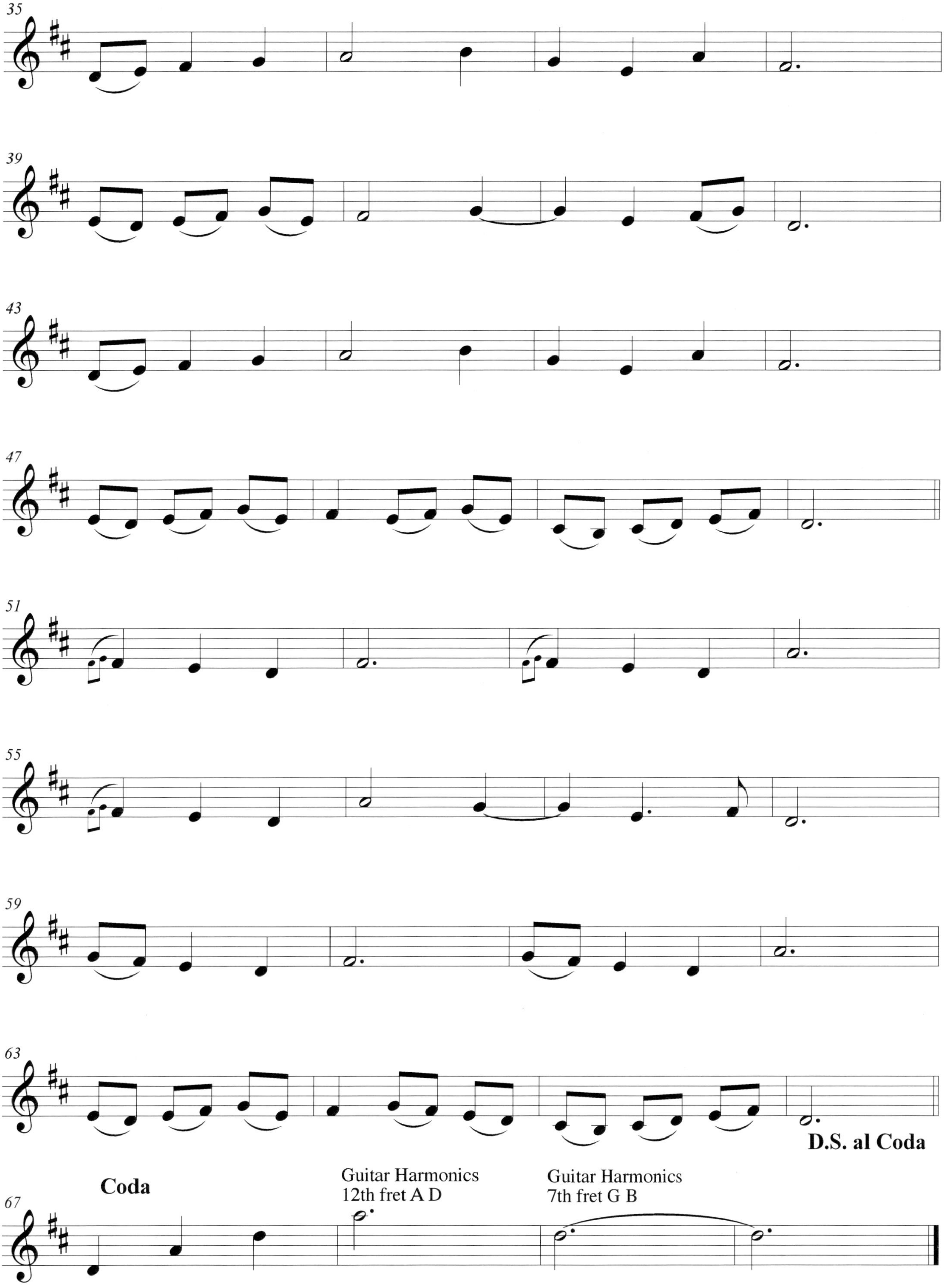

D.S. al Coda
Coda
Guitar Harmonics
12th fret A D
Guitar Harmonics
7th fret G B

43

Scotch Cap

Edinburgh Castle

John Playford 1651

♩. = 112-120

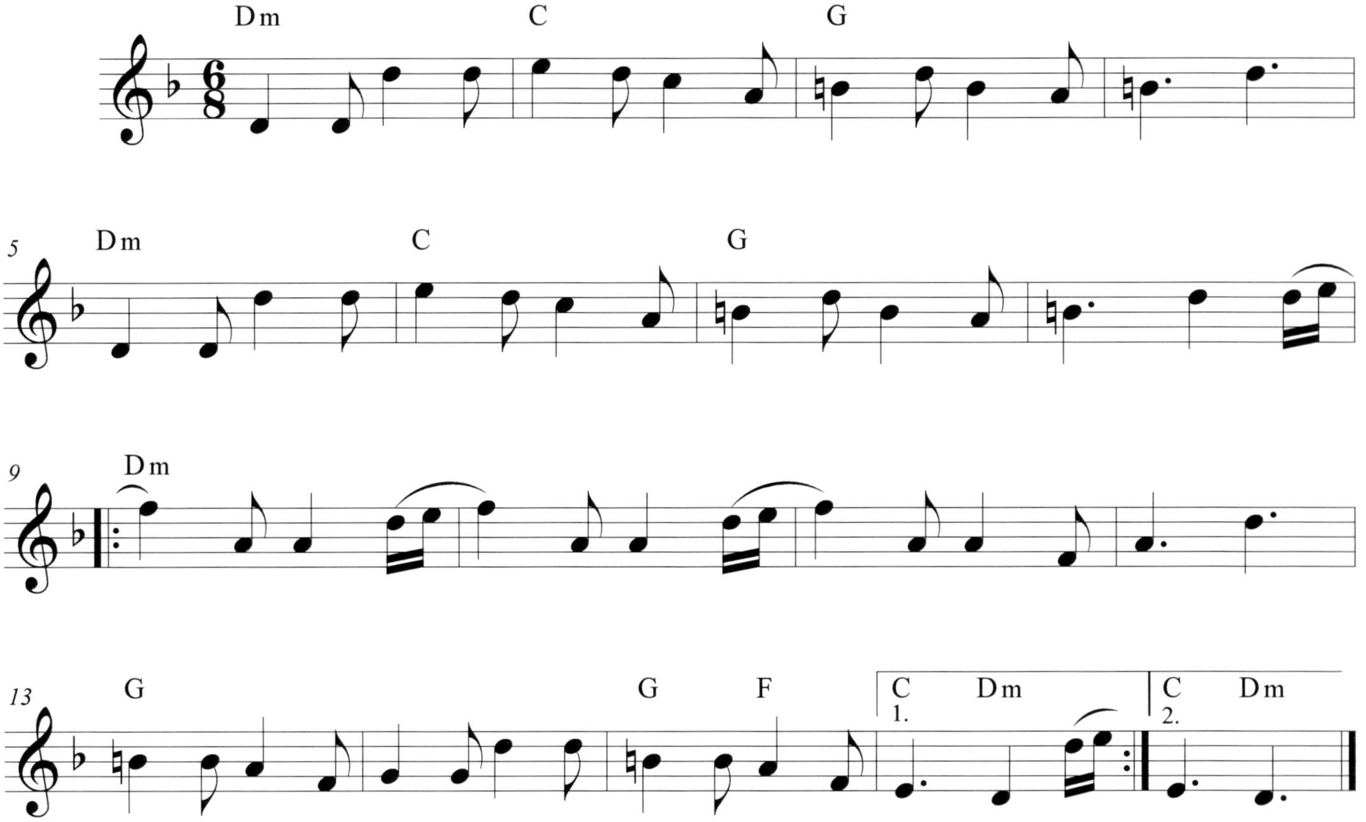

44

Woodicock

Whirligig

♩. = 112-140

John Playford 1651

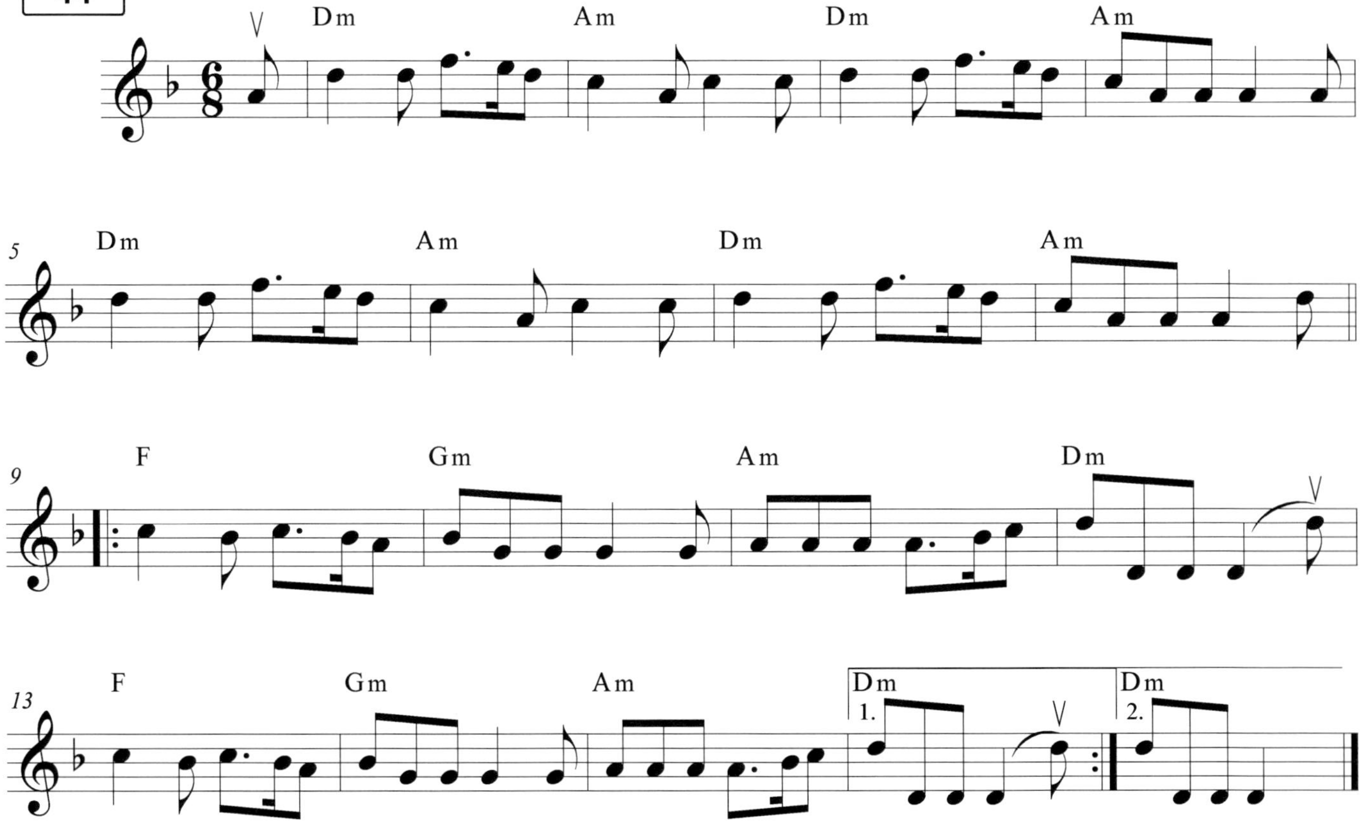

Sellenger's Round

The Beginning of the World

16 Century melody collected by
William Byrd and John Playford

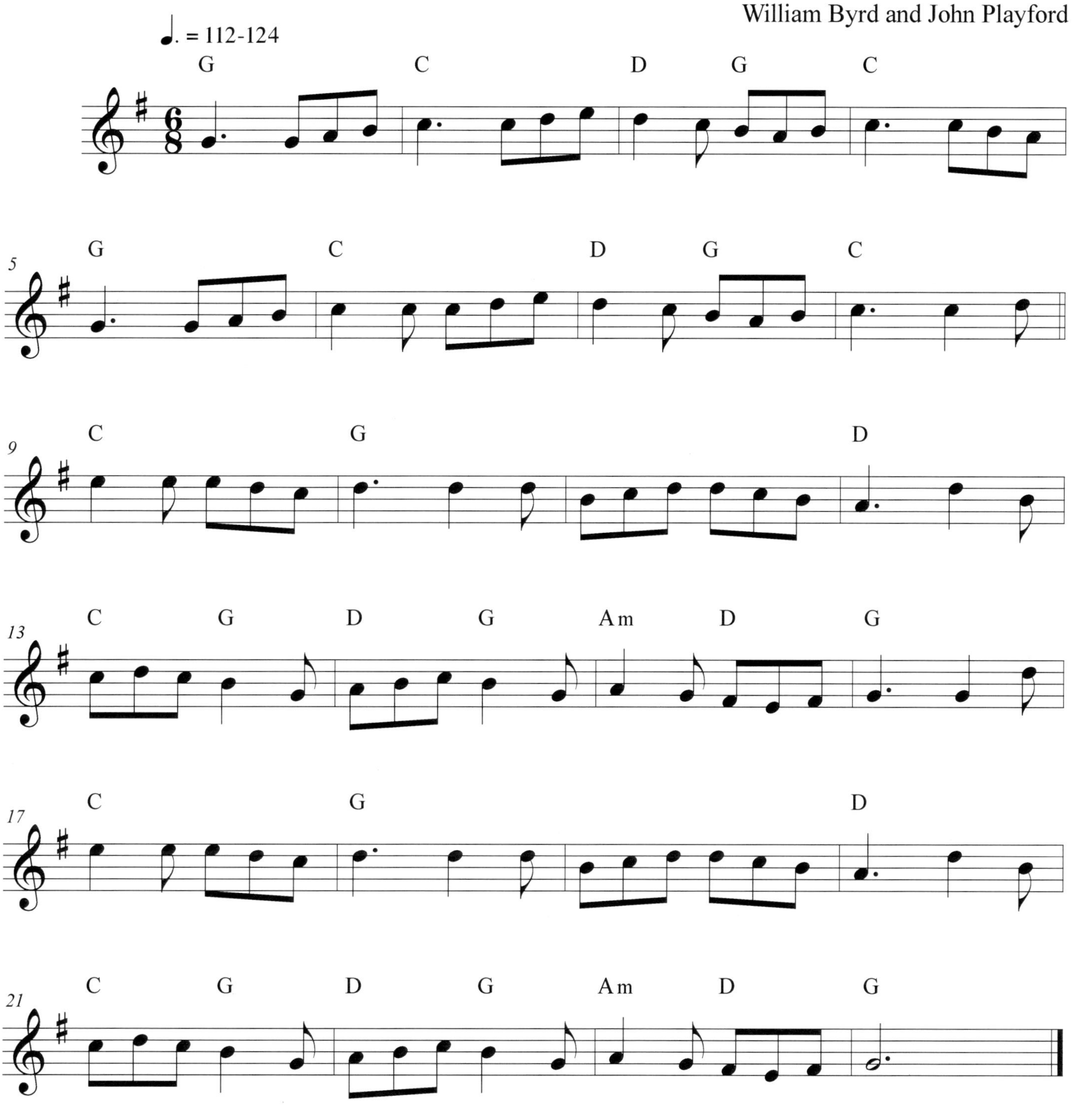

46

Step Stately

Jack Pudding

English Country Dance

𝅗𝅥 = 106-112

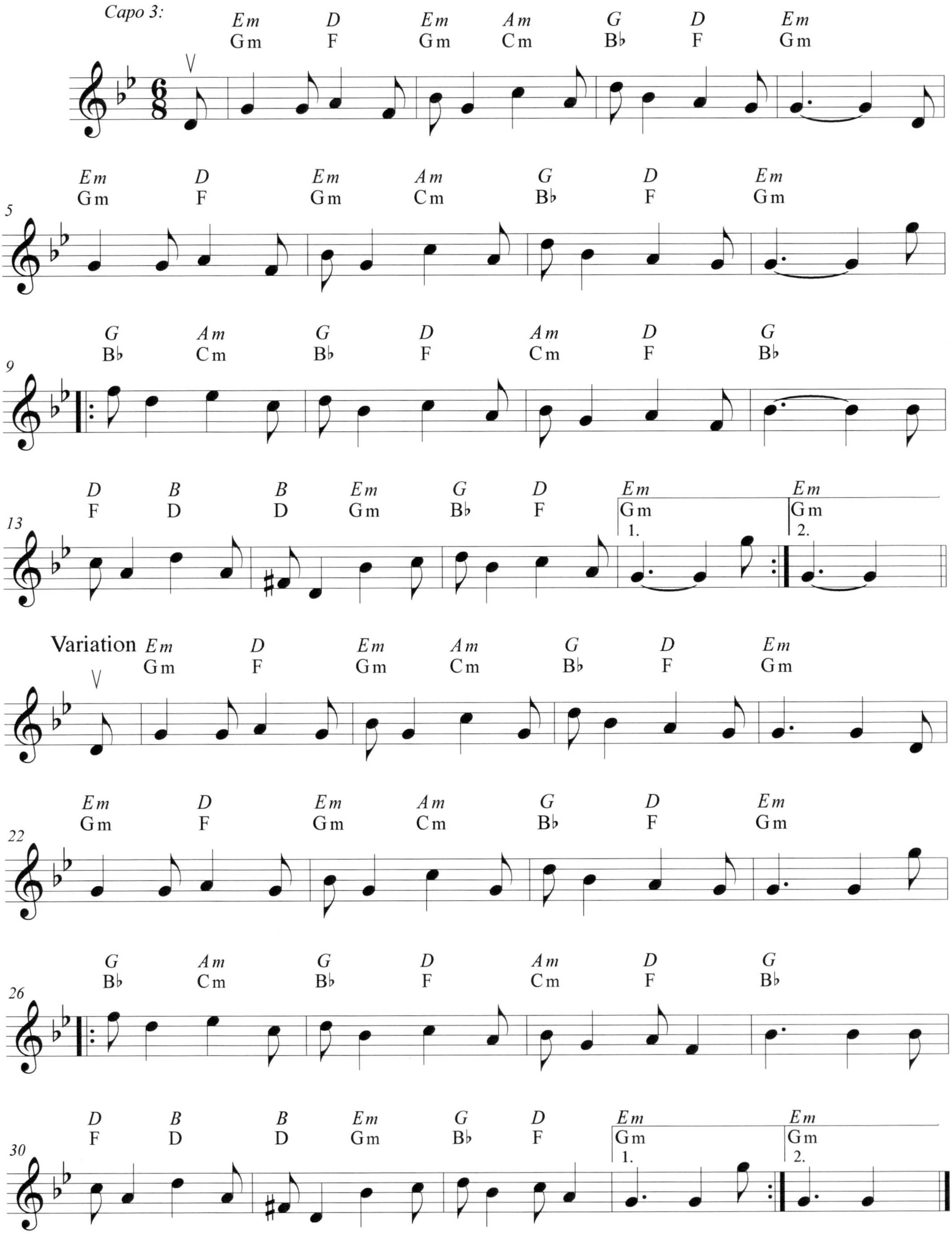

47

Well Hall

♩ = 110-122

John Playford 1679

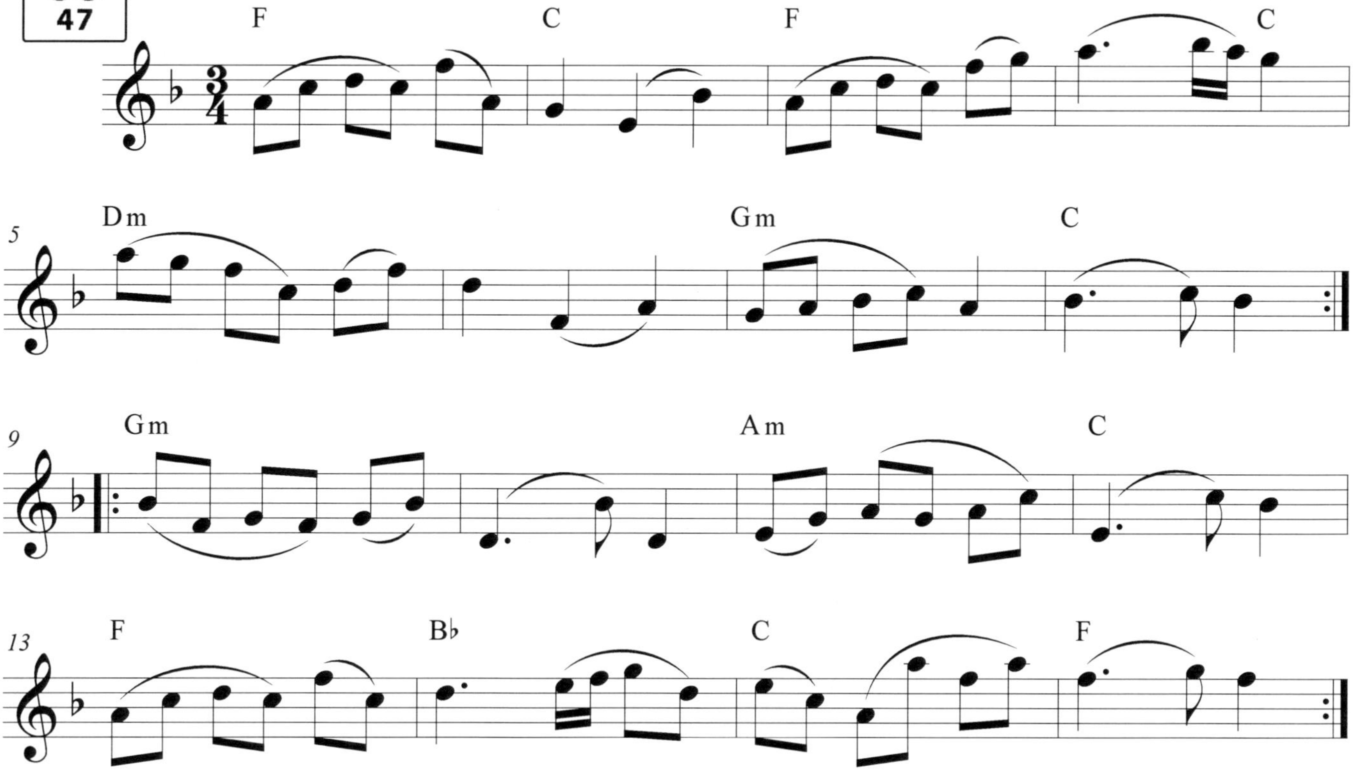

48

Wilson's Wilde

♩. = 50-60

Anonymous 16th Century

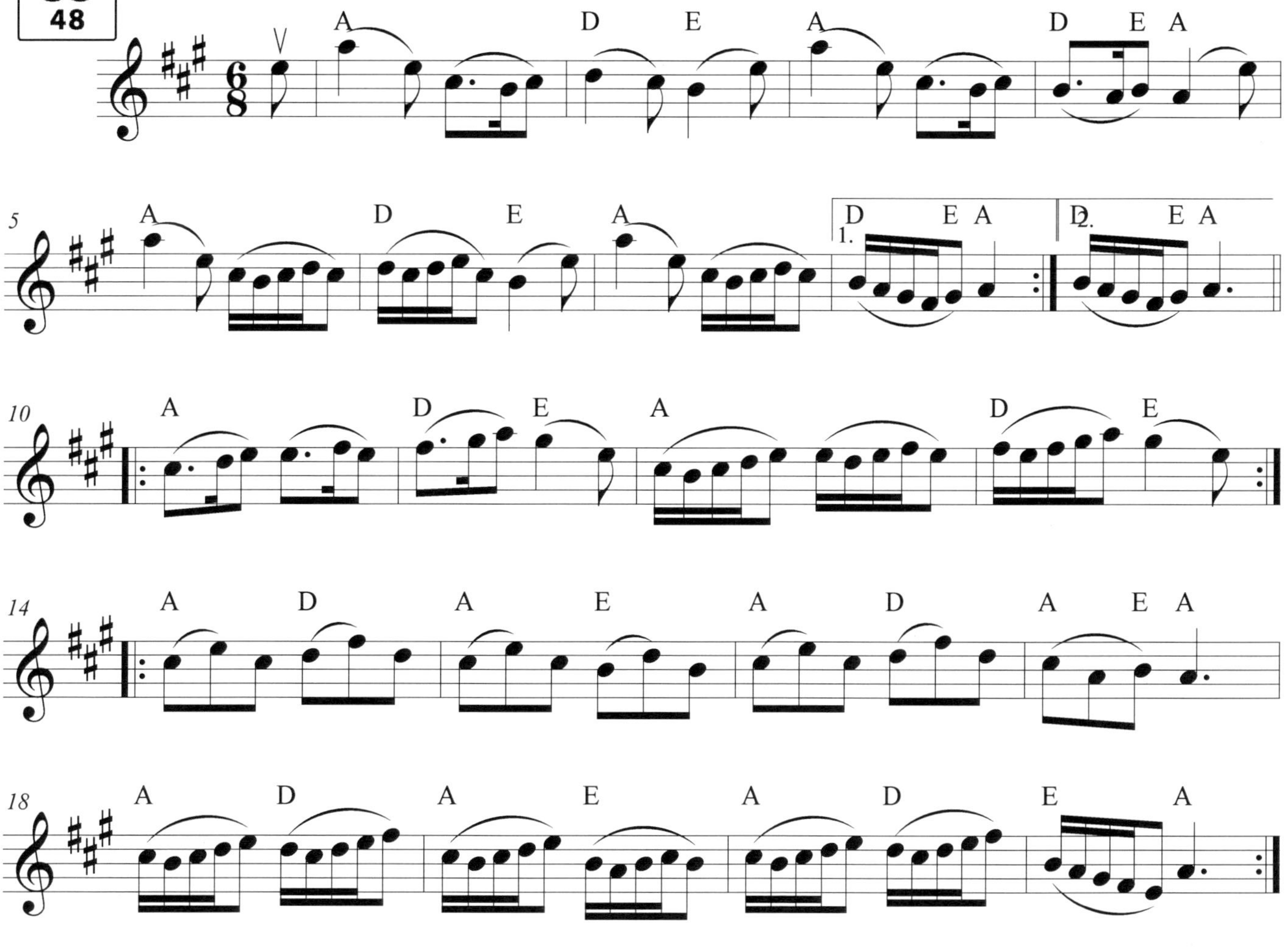

49

Westmorland

Westmoreland Waltz

The Dancing Master
John Playford 1686

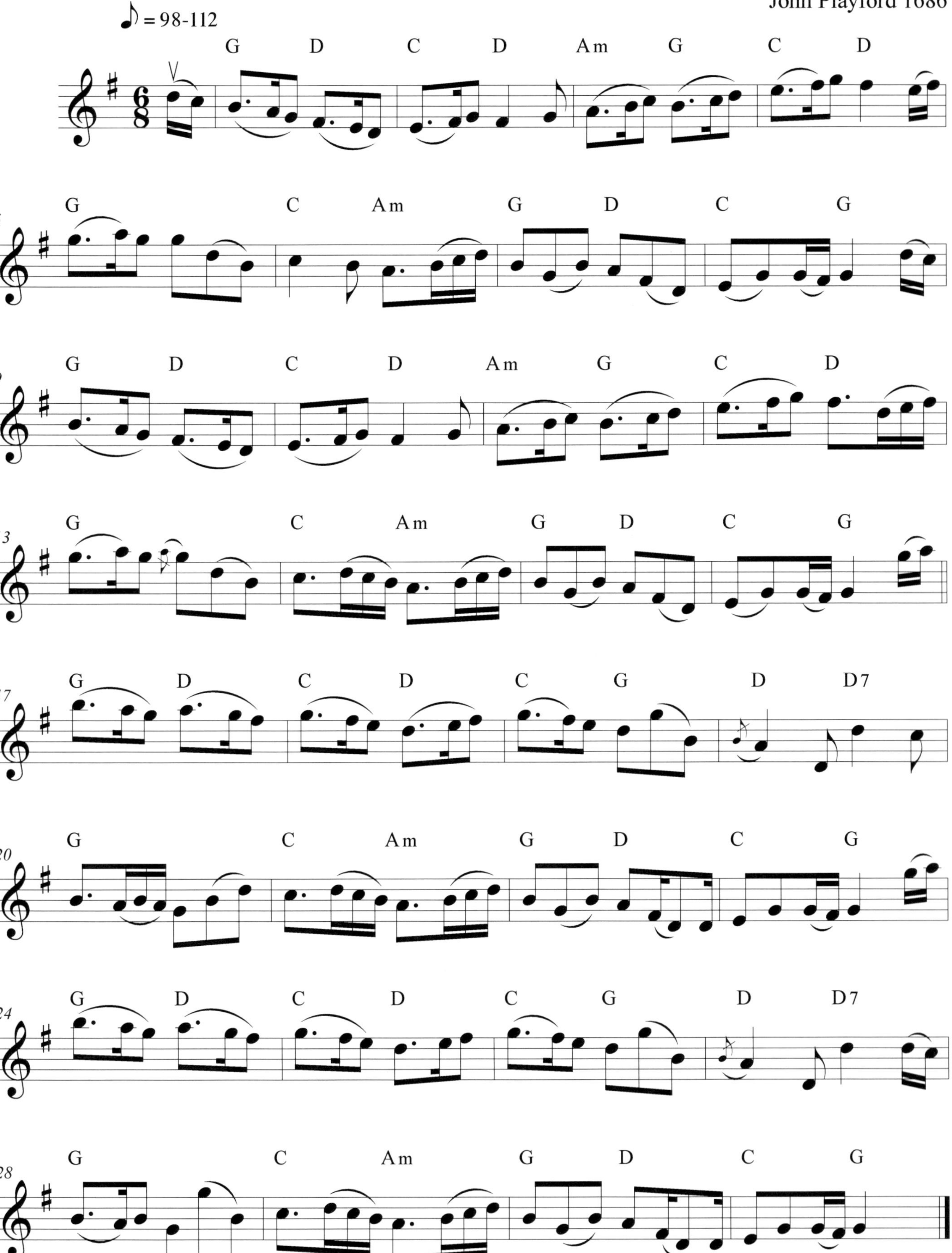